Azure and Xamarin Forms

Cross Platform Mobile Development

Russell Fustino

Apress®

Azure and Xamarin Forms: Cross Platform Mobile Development

Russell Fustino
New Port Richey, Florida, USA

ISBN-13 (pbk): 978-1-4842-3560-7   ISBN-13 (electronic): 978-1-4842-3561-4
https://doi.org/10.1007/978-1-4842-3561-4

Library of Congress Control Number: 2018947192

Managing Director, Apress Media LLC: Welmoed Spahr
Acquisitions Editor: Celestin Suresh John
Development Editor: James Markham
Coordinating Editor: Divya Modi

Cover designed by eStudioCalamar

Cover image designed by Freepik (www.freepik.com)

Distributed to the book trade worldwide by Springer Science+Business Media New York, 233 Spring Street, 6th Floor, New York, NY 10013. Phone 1-800-SPRINGER, fax (201) 348-4505, e-mail orders-ny@springer-sbm.com, or visit www.springeronline.com. Apress Media, LLC is a California LLC and the sole member (owner) is Springer Science+Business Media Finance Inc (SSBM Finance Inc). SSBM Finance Inc is a Delaware corporation.

For information on translations, please e-mail rights@apress.com, or visit www.apress.com/rights-permissions.

Apress titles may be purchased in bulk for academic, corporate, or promotional use. eBook versions and licenses are also available for most titles. For more information, reference our Print and eBook Bulk Sales web page at www.apress.com/bulk-sales.

Any source code or other supplementary material referenced by the author in this book is available to readers on GitHub via the book's product page, located at www.apress.com/978-1-4842-3560-7. For more detailed information, please visit www.apress.com/source-code.

Printed on acid-free paper

This book is dedicated to Nicholas, Justine, John, James, Olivia, and Melissa. It is also dedicated to my two brothers, Rich and Gary Fustino, and their families. They all inspire me, and I love them all dearly.

Table of Contents

About the Author

Russell Fustino is CEO of Fustino Brothers, Inc., makers of the endorsed "Jethro Tull" app, and a Microsoft MVP in Windows development. He is a former developer evangelist for Microsoft, as well as for Russ' ToolShed Network, Xamarin, Raygun, and ComponentOne. Russ is also a former Azure senior cloud solutions architect for Opsgility. He is highly experienced in developing cross platform apps using Xamarin and C# for UWP, Android, and iOS. Russ is a Xamarin Certified Mobile Developer. He has a passion for conveying relevant, current, and future software development technologies and tools through live seminars, teaching, and Internet video productions. Russ heads the Mobile Application Dev Tampa (www.MADTampa.com) user group in the Tampa, Florida, area. He is also the local PC handyman for his community, fixing viruses, providing tune-ups, and helping neighbors who have fallen prey to computer scams. Please like www.facebook.com/PCHandymanRussFustino/ and www.facebook.com/Fustinobrothers/ on Facebook. You can follow Russ on Twitter at @FustinoBrothers and @RussFustino and on LinkedIn at https://www.linkedin.com/in/russfustino/. Russ has enlightened, entertained, and educated more than 1 million developers in his career and is a recipient of the INETA (International .NET Association) Lifetime Achievement award.

About the Technical Reviewer

 **Sunny Mukherjee** is a software developer, architect, and mentor with a wealth of technical knowledge in various software disciplines, including ASP.NET, Web Services, Web API, Angular, WPF, Xamarin Forms, SQL, and Azure. He holds an MBA from the University of South Florida. He is always looking to bring value to technology solutions. In his personal time, he loves motorcycles, astronomy, movies, video games, exercising, meditation, and photography. If you want to learn about technology trends and career tips, you can follow his LinkedIn posts at www.linkedin.com/in/sunnymukherjee/.

Acknowledgments

I would like to acknowledge the Microsoft MVP program and community. Both have provided me years of networking with lots of great minds, as well as software that I use to run my business, not to mention incredible MVP Summits providing top-notch education. Joe Darko is my Program Manager Evangelist for MVPs in my neck of the woods, and his efforts are greatly appreciated. It's all about personalization and localization, and Joe gets that.

Introduction

It's as easy as 1-2-3. I often have been asked to recommend good books on getting started with Xamarin Forms or Azure or on how to use both tools. You are reading the book that I can now wholeheartedly recommend!

So, what exactly do I mean by "as easy as 1-2-3"? This refers to how this book will cover Azure and Xamarin Forms in depth, as no other book to date, specifically by means of the following steps:

1. Create a database for your app.

2. Serve up data in a service for the Xamarin Forms app to consume.

3. Consume the service from Azure in a Xamarin Forms app and display and/or update the data.

The preceding are the three steps in the Azure Mobile App Xamarin Forms Quick Start. They constitute my new "file new" when creating a future app. But wait, there's more! I will also cover both building a new app and modifying an existing app to Azure-ize it, including offline synchronization! If that is not enough, after reading this book, you should feel extremely comfortable using the Azure portal, with all the ins and outs of ramping up, and alleviate any related fears, including usage charges.

So why Xamarin Forms? To be honest, knowing C# and about 30 other languages, I simply did not want to learn Yet Another Language, YAL, with Objective-C, Java, Swift…and the list goes on. Not that I have anything against those languages, I just did not want to spend the time learning them. Time is too precious. Building apps that cross platforms is a necessity. For example, when I completed a Windows prototype version of the Jethro Tull fan app a few years ago, I said to my brothers, Rich and

Gary, "This app is a great fan app, and maybe we should actually show it to Jethro Tull." So, I sent an e-mail to Jethro Tull, with screenshots. Within six hours, they replied, "This looks great, do you also work with iPhone and Android"? Heck yah! We do now! Enter Xamarin.

My point is, in this day and age, you need apps for all of the platforms: Android, iOS, Windows. I could even imagine using Xamarin for more platforms on the horizon—for the Mac, watches, and other devices. Remember the slogan that propelled Java? "Write once. Run anywhere." Well, the saying lives on for C# and the .NET stack.

Let's talk about Xamarin and Xamarin Forms. Xamarin is the underlying platform that provides about 80 percent code-sharing. Xamarin Forms sits on top of the Xamarin platform, and it also shares the user interface layer. My Xamarin Forms apps typically provide 95 percent shared code. Let's say I am building a Windows UWP app with Xamarin Forms. When I am done with the UWP app, so will I be with the iOS and Android versions! No need to have three different skill sets and three sets of code from different languages. Only one skill set is required: Xamarin Forms and C#. When I worked as an evangelist for Xamarin, it was commonly said that anything you can do in Objective-C and Java, you can do with Xamarin. That's quite a statement, isn't it? It drove me to do deep-dive learning about Xamarin and get my Xamarin certification, that is for certain.

As for Azure, a common fear is cost. Be assured that there are many tools that I will cover in this book that can help you with this. When I was initially learning Azure, I felt it was an incredibly huge arena of technology. I now simply enjoy using Azure to build solutions, and it is easy to use as well. I have always been a proponent of third-party tools. Perhaps it was because third-party controls, for example, only require setting up a few properties, or calling some of the controls methods, and, presto, magic... you have created an app. Well, it is the same with setting properties on Azure blades. Once completed, you are well on your way to implementation. Azure just makes sense, period. The modern enterprise is cutting-edge and must be, to stay ahead of the competition.

Technology is advancing at an incredible rate. I sometimes think how I now program tasks, such as notifying millions of users simultaneously, using Azure, and it only takes a few lines of code. It is really mind-boggling. After reading this book, you will realize that Azure is a platform that is efficient, scalable, secure, easy-to-use, cost-effective, performant, well-documented, and well-supported. You will be surprised at how fast you can build your solutions from end-to-end with Azure and Xamarin Forms.

Enjoy the ride. I hope this book motivates you to begin a deep dive yourself. So, where do I focus my technology time without the fear of a white elephant? The answer: Azure and Xamarin Forms.

I am extremely honored to have written the first book combining two of today's hottest technologies for building cross platform apps and utilizing the cloud, via Azure and Xamarin Forms. The best news is that it's as easy as 1-2-3.

CHAPTER 1

Installing Visual Studio 2017

In this chapter, you will learn how to install Visual Studio 2017, which will be used to complete the examples in this book.

Note The source code and assets for this book can be downloaded from `https://github.com/Apress/azure-and-xamarin-forms`

Installing Visual Studio 2017 and Tools on Windows

This chapter covers how to install the required products to complete all the examples in this book.

- Windows 10 Pro or higher is required to run the emulators and cross platform development for iOS, Android, and Universal Windows Platform (UWP).

- Download and install Visual Studio Community 2017 or later versions, available at `www.visualstudio.com/thank-you-downloading-visual-studio/?sku=Community`.

© Russell Fustino 2018
R. Fustino, *Azure and Xamarin Forms*, https://doi.org/10.1007/978-1-4842-3561-4_1

- Select and install the UWP development workload, (Figure 1-1) under the Windows section, and Mobile development with .NET.

- Select the .NET (cross platform development using Xamarin) option, under the Mobile & Gaming section (Figure 1-2) on the Visual Studio (VS) 2017 Installer.

Figure 1-1. *Select Universal Windows Platform development*

Figure 1-2. *Select Mobile development with .NET*

Install ASP.NET and web development ➤ Azure development under the Web & Cloud section (Figure 1-3).

Web & Cloud (7)

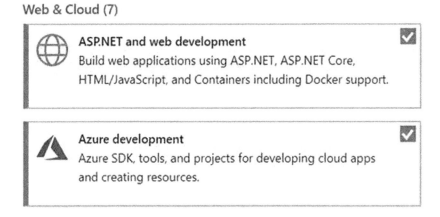

ASP.NET and web development
Build web applications using ASP.NET, ASP.NET Core, HTML/JavaScript, and Containers including Docker support.

Azure development
Azure SDK, tools, and projects for developing cloud apps and creating resources.

Figure 1-3. *Select ASP.NET and web development* ➤ *Azure development*

Install Data storage and processing, under the same section (Figure 1-4).

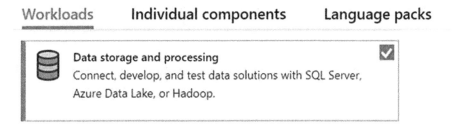

Workloads   **Individual components**   **Language packs**

Data storage and processing
Connect, develop, and test data solutions with SQL Server, Azure Data Lake, or Hadoop.

Figure 1-4. *Select Data storage and processing*

Under the Individual components tab, under the Emulators section, check off the following (Figure 1-5):

- Google Android Emulator (global)

- Intel Hardware Accelerated Execution Manager (global)

- Visual Studio Emulator for Android

- All Windows 10 Mobile Emulator (Anniversary Edition AND Creators Update)

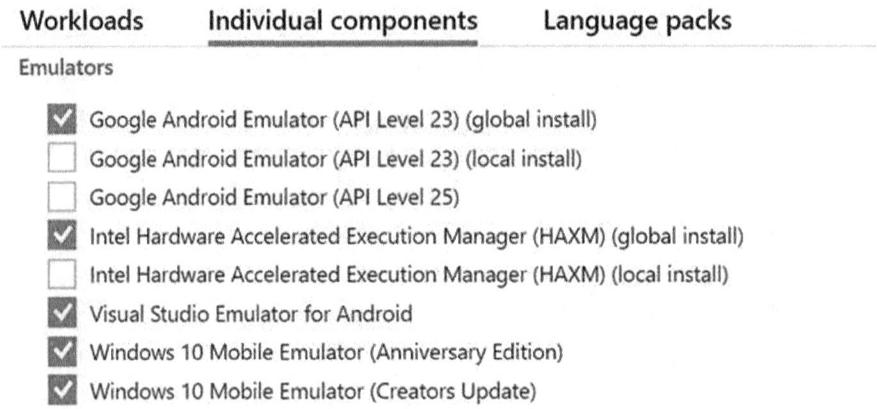

Workloads	**Individual components**	Language packs

Emulators

- ☑ Google Android Emulator (API Level 23) (global install)
- ☐ Google Android Emulator (API Level 23) (local install)
- ☐ Google Android Emulator (API Level 25)
- ☑ Intel Hardware Accelerated Execution Manager (HAXM) (global install)
- ☐ Intel Hardware Accelerated Execution Manager (HAXM) (local install)
- ☑ Visual Studio Emulator for Android
- ☑ Windows 10 Mobile Emulator (Anniversary Edition)
- ☑ Windows 10 Mobile Emulator (Creators Update)

Figure 1-5. *Select Google Android Emulator (global), Intel Hardware Accelerated Execution Manager (global), Visual Studio Emulator for Android, and Windows 10 Mobile Emulator (Anniversary Edition and Creators Update)*

If you do not see Google Android Emulator listed, this means that you do not have Hyper-V enabled. See Chapter 2 for how to enable Hyper-V. In the meantime, start the install.

Installing Visual Studio 2017 and Tools on the Mac

Optionally, install Visual Studio for the Mac. The purpose for a Mac installation would be to run, test, and deploy iOS and Android versions of your app in a Mac environment (UWP not supported). To build iOS apps on a PC, you must be wired to a Mac on the same network. Most of the examples in this book will use either the Android emulator or UWP local machine on a PC, so the Mac install is optional for the book. Instructions are available at https://developer.xamarin.com/guides/ios/getting_started/installation/mac/.

Other Tools

- Postman (`www.getpostman.com` and install)

- SQL Server Management Studio (`https://docs.microsoft.com/en-us/sql/ssms/download-sql-server-management-studio-ssms`). This tool will be used to verify our database contents.

- Firefox (`www.mozilla.org/firefox/new/`). Firefox has a nicely formatted view when looking at JSON data coming back from a web service.

Summary

In this chapter, you learned how to install Visual Studio 2017, which will be used to complete the examples in this book, and some other tools, such as Postman, SQL Server Management Studio, and Firefox. Visual Studio for the Mac is an optional installation. In the next chapter, we will build a Xamarin Forms app.

CHAPTER 2

Introduction to Xamarin Forms

Xamarin Forms is an awesome cross platform environment from which to build iOS, Android, and UWP apps, as well as other potential platforms in the future.

Project Overview

In this chapter, you'll get your feet wet with Xamarin Forms via five projects. Each project builds on the prior one. Several topics will be covered in this introductory chapter, including how to create a Xamarin Forms solution, as well as emulator tips, navigation, images, event handlers, device form factors, and list views. The result will be a typical app with a main navigation page, a list view page, and a detail page that you can use as a template for building future apps! We will be creating a book list project that has a main navigation page that looks like that in Figure 2-1.

© Russell Fustino 2018
R. Fustino, *Azure and Xamarin Forms*, https://doi.org/10.1007/978-1-4842-3561-4_2

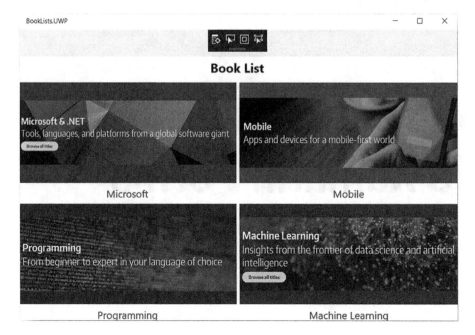

Figure 2-1. *Main navigation page in the completed project*

It has a list view page that looks like that in Figure 2-2.

Figure 2-2. *ListView page in the completed project*

The app will navigate to a detail page on the Apress site for the book selected from a list such as that in Figure 2-3.

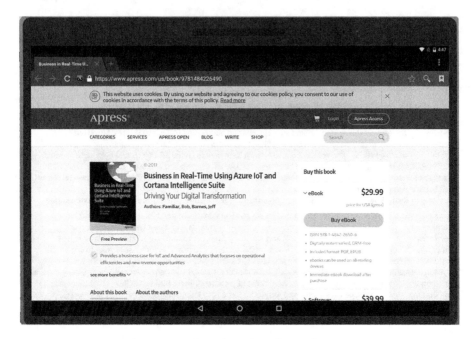

Figure 2-3. *Detail page in the completed project*

- We'll first create a new Xamarin Forms application and review the structure of the solution. We'll then run the application for Android, UWP, and, optionally, iOS, if connected with a Mac server. As this is a cross platform app, you can use any mix of the platform projects, depending on your development environment (Mac or Windows).

- We will then enhance the app, to have a main navigation page, with `StackLayout` and `GridLayout`, which considers device form factors for phones and tablets, using device-specific logic.

- We will use XAML and code behind to control your layout form factors for tablets and phones.

- We will also use embedded resource images of the MainPage.

- A ListView page will be added with a selection event handler. You can also run these examples on Visual Studio (VS) for Mac; however, this does not support UWP.

Note   Run all the exercises in this book from your laptop/PC and not an Azure virtual machine.

Time Estimate

70 Minutes

Project 2-1: Creating Your First Xamarin Forms Application

Time Estimate

20 Minutes

In this project, you will create your first Xamarin Forms application. You will see how to get started in Visual Studio 2017 and build a Xamarin Forms application by choosing a built-in template to get stated with. Then you will get your emulators working and add a page and navigate between the two.

1. Start Visual Studio 2017. Sign in with the same credentials as your Azure or developer account. Figure 2-4 shows Sign in.

Figure 2-4. *Visual Studio Welcome screen sign in*

    2.   From the File menu, select New ➤ Project. See
          Figure 2-5.

Start Page - Microsoft Visual Studio								
File	Edit	View	Project	Incredibuild	Debug	Team	Tools	Architecture	Test

```
New                              ▶    Project...
Open                             ▶    Web Site...
Start Page                            Repository...
Close                                 File...
Close Solution                        Project From Existing Code...
Save Selected Items    Ctrl+S         Import
```

Figure 2-5. *Visual Studio File ➤ New ➤ Project*

3. Expand Templates ➤ Visual C# ➤ Cross-Platform
    and select Cross Platform App and use **BookLists**
    as the Name at a location near your root **(C\Demo)**.
    It is always advisable to select a Location near your
    root, as Android will often complain about the file
    path being too long. See Figure 2-6.

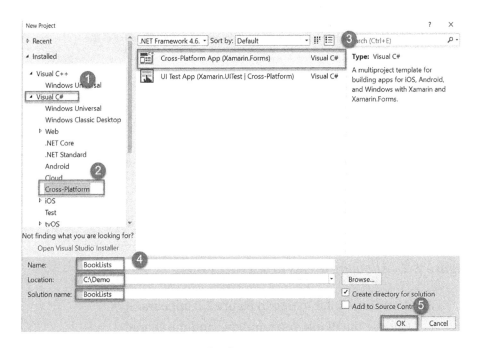

Figure 2-6. *Open the Cross-Platform Xamarin.Forms*
application template.

4. If you get prompted by a Windows Security Alert, select both the private and public options and click Allow access. See Figure 2-7.

Figure 2-7. *Allowing access to a security alert*

5. A screen similar to that in Figure 2-8 appears. Choose the Blank App template, and the shared .NET Standard Code Sharing Strategy options. Then click OK.

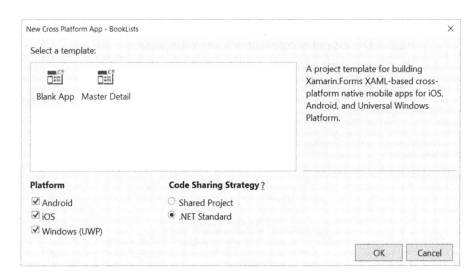

Figure 2-8. *Choosing the Blank App template, and the .NET Standard Code Sharing Strategy options*

6. If prompted for UWP versions, accept the defaults
    and click OK. See Figure 2-9.

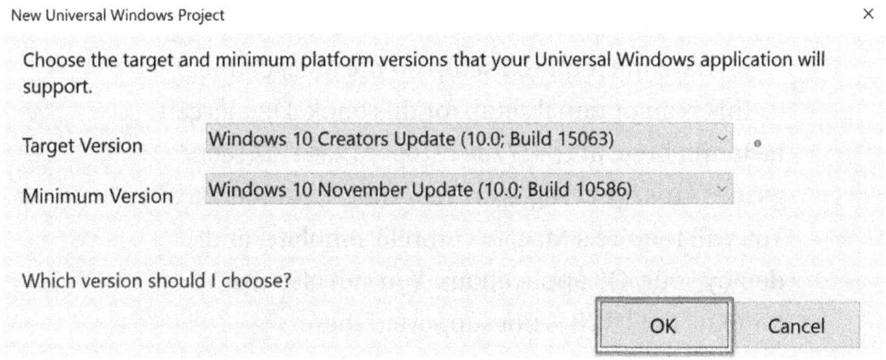

Figure 2-9. *Accepting the defaults for Target Version and Minimum Version UWP application support*

7. If prompted to use the User developer features, select Developer mode when your settings are displayed. This will allow you to deploy to devices. See Figure 2-10.

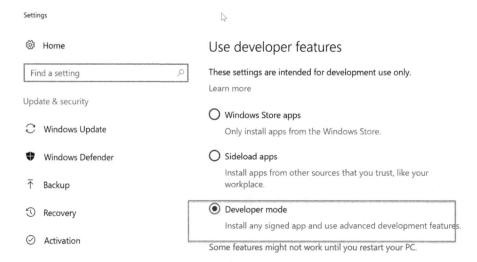

Figure 2-10. *If prompted, select Developer mode in your settings*

8. If you are prompted for the Mac Server, ignore it or, if you have the required setup on the Mac, connect it. This is an optional setup for this book. Details can be found here: `https://developer.xamarin.com/guides/ios/getting_started/installation/mac/`. You will require a Mac, to compile, emulate, and deploy your iOS applications. You can also use VS for Mac, but UWP is not supported there.

9. Review the solution architecture in the Solution Explorer window (Figure 2-11). You will see four projects in this solution: one for each of the head projects—Android, iOS, and Universal Windows (UWP)—and one for shared projects. The head projects are for your startup projects to select from, depending on which platform you want to run. The shared .NET Standard project is where you will put most of your code. This could be more than 95 percent.

Figure 2-11. *Solution Explorer contains shared, Android, iOS, and UWP projects*

10. Select BookLists.Android as the project you wish to run, right-click it, and select Set as StartUp Project, as shown in Figure 2-12.

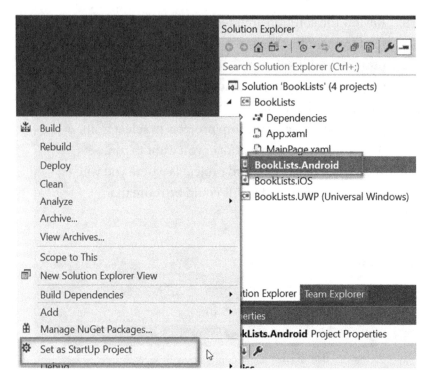

Figure 2-12. *Android Set as StartUp Project*

Note   You will see the sections "Try{…}" and "Catch{…}" in among the following steps.

In code, we often use `Try/Catch` in error-handling. For those of you who are unfamiliar with this, try some code, and if it does not work, handle it in the `Catch` clause.

In instructions throughout this book, you also may see these terms without text in braces following. In such cases, the terms suggest that you try something, and if this does not work, to check the `Catch` section(s) that immediately follow, for a possible solution.

11. **Try:** Run the app, selecting the emulator for the 5" KitKat. The emulators that begin with the size of the device are the VS 2017 Android emulators. These are the fastest Android emulators. See Figure 2-13.

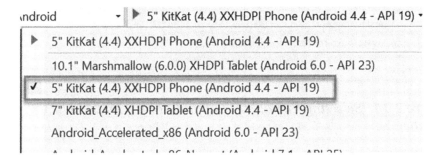

Figure 2-13. 5" KitKat selected

12. **Catch:** If you do not see the VS 2017 Android emulators, you will have to run the VS 2017 Installer Program, modify it for your installed version, and select the Individual Components tab. Scroll down until you see the Emulators section. Check Visual Studio Emulator for Android. This will take several minutes to install, and you may have to reboot. See Figure 2-14.

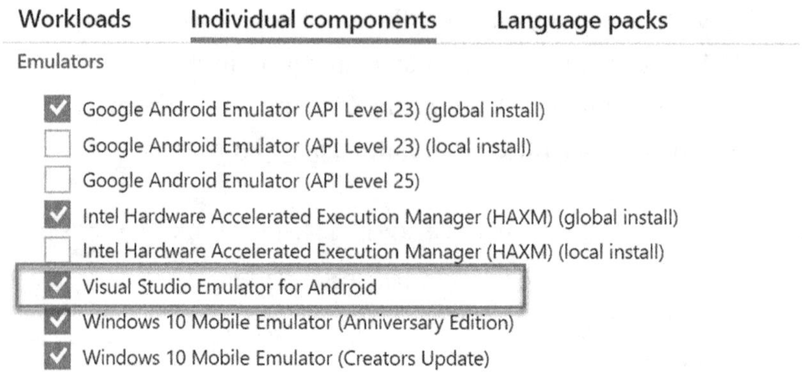

Workloads	Individual components	Language packs

Emulators

☑ Google Android Emulator (API Level 23) (global install)
☐ Google Android Emulator (API Level 23) (local install)
☐ Google Android Emulator (API Level 25)
☑ Intel Hardware Accelerated Execution Manager (HAXM) (global install)
☐ Intel Hardware Accelerated Execution Manager (HAXM) (local install)
☑ Visual Studio Emulator for Android
☑ Windows 10 Mobile Emulator (Anniversary Edition)
☑ Windows 10 Mobile Emulator (Creators Update)

Figure 2-14. Selecting Visual Studio Emulator for Android in VS Installer

13. **Catch:** {If you do not see the Visual Studio Emulator for Android in the list, this means that you are not running Hyper-V. To run Hyper-V, you must change your bios settings to support virtualization. Close all applications. Right-click the start button and select Run. Type "shutdown/r/o." This will reboot your machine with options and allow you to troubleshoot advanced options, to bring up the firmware settings for the bios. Once in the bios, use the arrow keys to navigate to the desired section and look for an option to enable virtualization. Then repeat the step above.} See Figures 2-15 and 2-16.

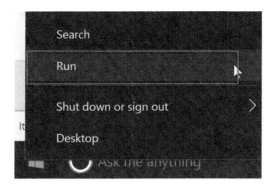

Figure 2-15. *Right-click Start and select Run*

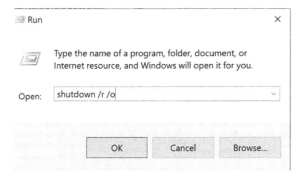

Figure 2-16. *Type "shutdown/r/o" to restart with options*

14. **Catch:** {Some machines are too fast for the emulator. If your app starts in the VS Android emulator but exits quickly, perform the following steps (Android app starts and immediately closes, debugging stops):

    a. Close the Android simulator window, to shut down the virtual machine.

    b. Go to the properties of the Android project, hit tab Android options, and unselect Use Fast Deployment.

21

   c. Start Hyper-V Manager (This is the Microsoft program to manage virtual machines in Windows; you have it installed.)

   d. Select the emulator you are trying to use. If the desired emulator does not appear, you must either launch it first from either Visual Studio or from the Visual Studio Emulator for Android.

   e. Right-click for context menu, then hit Settings.

   f. In the Settings dialog, expand Processor.

   g. Click Compatibility.

   h. In the right pane set check box "Migrate to a physical computer with a different processor version"

   i. Start the debugging in Visual Studio to restart the simulator.}See Figure 2-17.

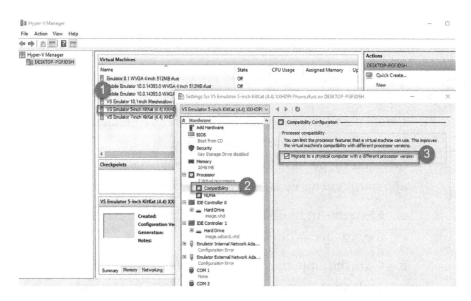

Figure 2-17. *In Hyper-V Manager, select the emulator that ends the app quickly, select Settings ➤ Compatibility, and check the Migrate option*

15. Rotate the phone, slide the lock to unlock it, and
     you should see "Welcome to Xamarin Forms." See
     Figures 2-18 and 2-19.

Figure 2-18. *Selecting the rotate to right button and sliding up the lock*

Figure 2-19. *Your first app appears in Android, using Xamarin Forms!*

16. Now right-click and select the UWP project and make it the Startup project. See Figure 2-20.

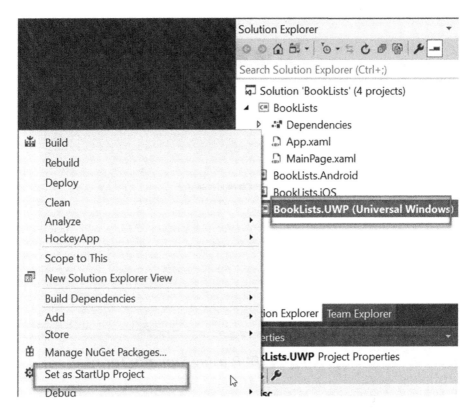

Figure 2-20. *Select UWP as the Startup project*

17. **Try:** Run the app on the Local Machine. See
     Figures 2-21 and 2-22.

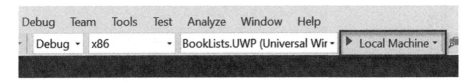

Figure 2-21. *Selecting Local Machine*

Figure 2-22. *Your first app on UWP, using Xamarin Forms*

18. **Catch:** {The first time you go to run a project on
    UWP, you may have to check the build configuration
    first and make sure that the deploy and build
    options are checked and are x64. Under the Build
    menu, select Configuration Manager...}
    See Figures 2-23 and 2-24.

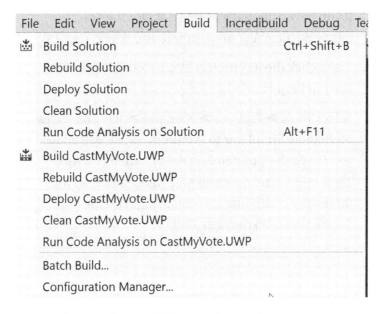

Figure 2-23. *Selecting the Build ➤ Configuration Manager... option*

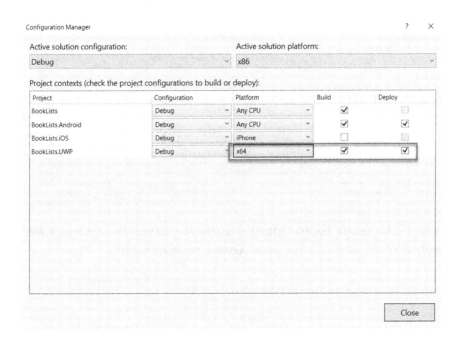

Figure 2-24. *Selecting Build and Deploy for UWP*

19. If you have optionally installed VS for the Mac, follow the next few steps; otherwise, skip to step 25.

20. Right-click the iOS project in the solution and set as Startup Project.

21. Select Tools ➤ Options ➤ Xamarin ➤ iOS and check off Remote Simulator to Windows, which will allow you to see the simulator on the PC when you run. Then select Find Xamarin Mac Agent and read the three-step procedure for remote login on the Mac. See Figures 2-25 through 2-28.

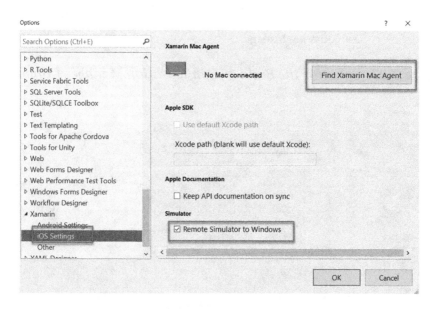

Figure 2-25. *Select Tools, Options, Xamarin, and iOS Settings. Check Remote Simulator and click Find Xamarin Mac Agent.*

Figure 2-26. *Step 1 of 3 for Remote Login*

Figure 2-27. *Step 2 of 3 for Remote Login*

Figure 2-28. *Step 3 of 3 for Remote Login*

22. On the Mac, find the IP address by clicking the
    Apple logo in the upper-left corner and then select
    System Preferences and Network. Copy the IP
    address. Back on the PC, click Add Server and enter
    the Mac IP address. You will be prompted for your
    username and password on the Mac. You should see
    the connection machine turn green. See Figure 2-29.

Figure 2-29. *Select Add Server, or Connect, if you have a previous
connection*

23. To run in the iOS simulator, select iPhoneSimulator, the small drop-down arrow will provide a list of simulators. Select iPhone 8 iOS. You may have to close the simulator once, if it does not start up the first time in a minute or two, and rerun. (See Figures 2-30 and 2-31.) If the simulator does not appear, know that it sometimes runs behind your Visual Studio window. So just move windows around till you see it, or cycle through your open apps using an Alt+Tab key combination.

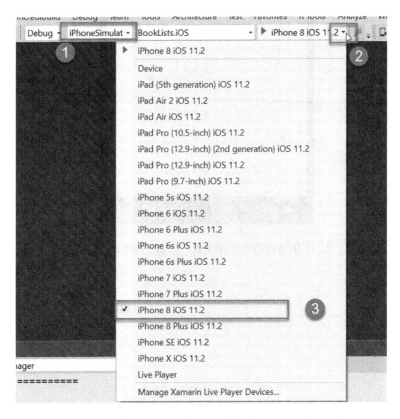

Figure 2-30. *Select iPhoneSimulator (1), the tiny drop-down arrow (2), and the simulator model, such as iPhone 8 iOS (3)*

31

Figure 2-31. *The iPhoneSimulator displays running the app*

24. Stop the app. Add a new page to the shared .NET
Standard project. Right-click the shared .NET
Standard project, select Add ➤ New Item. See
Figure 2-32.

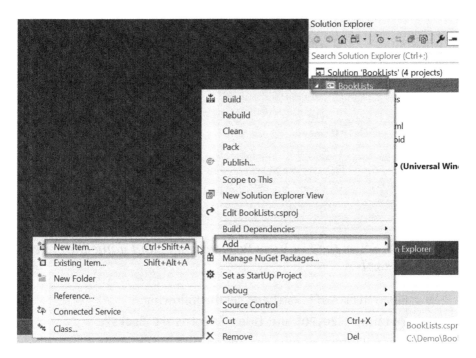

Figure 2-32. *Right-click BookLists and select Add ➤ New Item....*

25. Select Visual C# Items ➤ List View Page and name
the page `Microsoft.xaml.` See Figure 2-33.

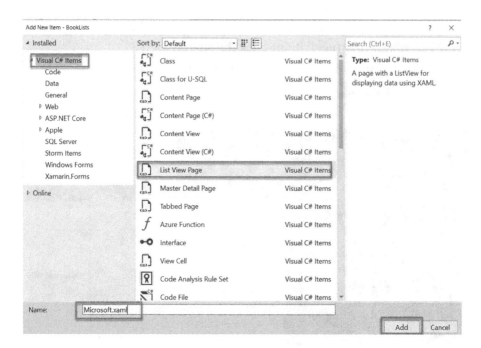

Figure 2-33. *Select the List View Page template and name the page*
`Microsoft.xaml`

26. Open `Microsoft.xaml` and set the following:
    Padding = "20,20" and Title = "`Microsoft Books`".
    This will provide some spacing around the children
    views of the content page and give it a title. Always
    use double quotes around values in XAML. See
    Figure 2-34.

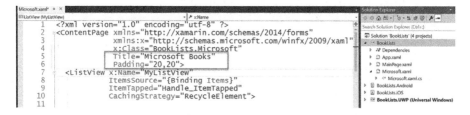

Figure 2-34. *Add Title =* "`Microsoft Books`" *and Padding =* "`20,20`"

27. In Solution Explorer, double-click the `MainPage.xaml` page in the shared .NET Standard project, to see the XAML. Also, note that when you expand the XAML page, there is a code behind file associated with it in Solution Explorer. See Figure 2-35.

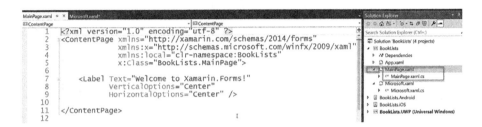

Figure 2-35. *Each XAML file has a related code behind the `xaml.cs` file*

28. Replace the Label view with a `StackLayout` that contains a button with the following markup.

Replace this

```
<Label Text="Welcome to Xamarin.Forms!"
        VerticalOptions="Center"
        HorizontalOptions="Center" />
```

with this

```
<StackLayout>
    <Button Margin="20,20"
            WidthRequest="100"
            Text="Press to see ListView Page">
    </Button>
</StackLayout>
```

Note   Newer versions of Visual Studio may already have the StackLayout on the default template. If so, just replace the Label with the Button and keep the existing StackLayout.

---

29. Now add a clicked event to the button...

Your code should now look like this in `MainPage.xaml`:

```
<StackLayout>
    <Button Margin="20,20"
            WidthRequest="100"
            Text="Press to see ListView Page"
            Clicked="MicrosoftBooks_Clicked">
    </Button>
</StackLayout>
```

30. Open the code behind page, `MainPage.xaml.cs,` and add an event handler for `MicrosoftBooks_Clicked` after the MainPage constructor, if one is not already there, as follows:

```
using System;
using System.Collections.Generic;
using System.Linq;
using System.Text;
using System.Threading.Tasks;
using Xamarin.Forms;
```

```
namespace BookLists
{
        public partial class MainPage : ContentPage
        {
                public MainPage()
                {
                        InitializeComponent();
                }

        private void MicrosoftBooks_Clicked(object
        sender, EventArgs e)
        {
            Navigation.PushAsync(new Microsoft());
        }

    }
}
```

31. Open App.xaml.cs and comment out the code
    to start the MainPage and replace it by starting a
    NavigationPage. You can find pages in the solution
    by typing in the search window in Solution Explorer.
    Here you see two app.xaml files: one in the shared
    .NET Standard project, and one in the UWP project.
    The user interface (UI) code goes in the shared .NET
    Standard project. See Figure 2-36.

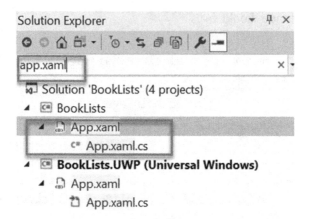

Figure 2-36. *Searching on app.xaml in Solution Explorer yields two sets. Use the one in BookLists.*

```
public App ()
{
                InitializeComponent();

    // MainPage = new BookLists.MainPage();

    MainPage = new NavigationPage(new
    MainPage());
}
```

32. Select the UWP head project, or whichever head project you desire as the Startup project. Run the app, and you should be able to navigate to the ListPage and back to the MainPage.

33. Open MainPage.xaml and modify the text property to "Microsoft Books"

```
<StackLayout>
    <Button Margin=" 20,20"
        Text="Microsoft Books"
        Clicked="MicrosoftBooks_Clicked">
    </Button>
</StackLayout>
```

34. Run the app and click the Microsoft Books button. Then navigate to the Microsoft Books ListView page. See Figure 2-37.

Figure 2-37. *See the home Navigation page* `MainPage.xaml`

35. You should see the Microsoft Books ListView page and a list of items, as well as a tapped event handler, when you click on an item. See Figure 2-38.

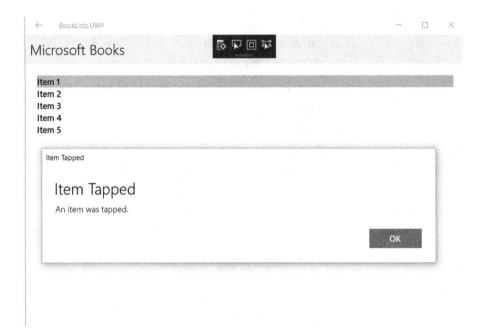

Figure 2-38. *By selecting Item, you will see a message that an item was tapped*

Congratulations! You have just created your first Xamarin app.

Project 2-2: Working with the User Interface

Time Estimate

15 Minutes

In this project, you will create a user interface (UI) and employ the StackLayout and GridLayout classes. These are very popular building blocks for your UI. StackLayout flows similarly to an HTML page, with UI items that relate to each other, in a vertical or horizontal stack, for example. GridLayout is useful for layouts that are best defined by rows and columns. For example,

StackLayout might be good for the phone, as you typically scroll up and down in a phone app, whereas GridLayout might be good for a tablet, to help users take advantage of all the additional real estate on the device.

1. Continue with the same app. We will now place four buttons on the main page. Replace the StackLayout markup XAML in MainPage.xaml with the following markup:

```
<StackLayout>
  <Button Margin="20,20"
      WidthRequest="100"
      Text="Microsoft Books"
      Clicked="MicrosoftBooks_Clicked">
  </Button>
  <Button Margin="20,20"
      WidthRequest="100"
      Text="Programming"
      Clicked="Programming_Clicked">
  </Button>
  <Button Margin="20,20"
      WidthRequest="100"
      Text="Mobile"
      Clicked="Mobile_Clicked">
  </Button>
  <Button Margin="20,20"
      WidthRequest="100"
      Text="Machine Learning"
      Clicked="MachineLearning_Clicked">
  </Button>
</StackLayout>
```

2. Create clicked event handlers for each button and
    leave the new handlers empty for now, as follows in
    MainPage.xaml.cs:

```
namespace BookLists
{
    public partial class MainPage : ContentPage
    {
        public MainPage()
        {
            InitializeComponent();
        }

        private void MicrosoftBooks_Clicked(object
        sender, EventArgs e)
        {
            Navigation.PushAsync(new Microsoft());
        }
        private void Programming_Clicked(object sender,
        EventArgs e)
        {

        }
        private void Mobile_Clicked(object sender,
        EventArgs e)
        {

        }
        private void MachineLearning_Clicked(object
        sender, EventArgs e)
        {

        }
    }
}
```

3. In a stack layout, the children are displayed in the
    order they appear in the XAML. Also, the default
    StackLayout orientation is vertical. Run the app,
    and you should see the buttons listed vertically, as
    in Figure 2-39.

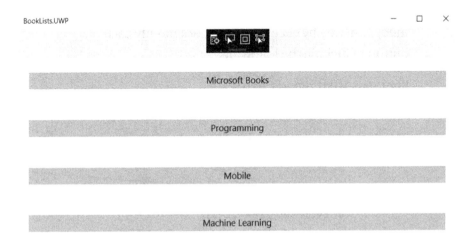

Figure 2-39. *All the new buttons are displayed*

4. You may be wondering why the buttons stretch
    across the width of the page, although we
    have specified WidthRequest only to 100. That
    is because the default value for StackLayout
    HorizontalOptions with a vertical orientation is
    FillAndExpand. These sizes are not pixels. Instead,
    they are device-independent units recognized
    independently by each platform. Let's modify each
    button to include the following:

```
HorizontalOptions="Center"
WidthRequest ="300"
```

This StackLayout XAML should look like the
following:

```
<StackLayout>
    <Button Margin="20,20"
            WidthRequest="300"
            HorizontalOptions="Center"
            Text="Microsoft Books"
            Clicked="MicrosoftBooks_Clicked">
            </Button>
    <Button Margin="20,20"
            WidthRequest="300"
            HorizontalOptions="Center"
            Text="Programming"
            Clicked="Programming_Clicked"></Button>
    <Button Margin="20,20"
            WidthRequest="300"
            HorizontalOptions="Center"
            Text="Mobile"
            Clicked="Mobile_Clicked"></Button>
```

```
<Button Margin="20,20"
        WidthRequest="300"
        HorizontalOptions="Center"
        Text="Machine Learning"
        Clicked="MachineLearning_Clicked">
        </Button>
</StackLayout>
```

5. Now run it to see the resized buttons in Figure 2-40.

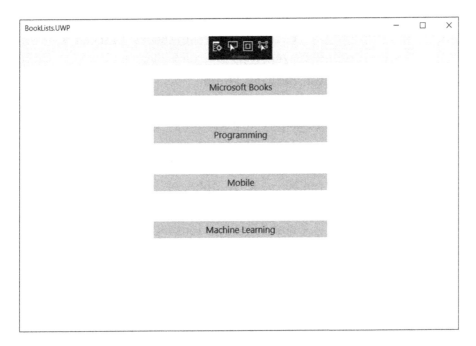

Figure 2-40. *Buttons are now displayed centered, with a width of 300*

6. Comment out the StackLayout XAML, as we will
    use this later. To comment out a section of code
    in Visual Studio, select the desired code that you
    want to comment and then press CTRL+K and then
    CTRL+C. (To uncomment, use CTRL+K, CTRL+U.)

```xml
<!--<StackLayout>
    <Button Margin="20,20"
            WidthRequest="300"
            HorizontalOptions="Center"
            Text="Microsoft Books"
            Clicked="MicrosoftBooks_Clicked">
            </Button>
    <Button Margin="20,20"
            WidthRequest="300"
            HorizontalOptions="Center"
            Text="Programming"
            Clicked="Programming_Clicked"></Button>
    <Button Margin="20,20"
            WidthRequest="300"
            HorizontalOptions="Center"
            Text="Mobile"
            Clicked="Mobile_Clicked"></Button>
    <Button Margin="20,20"
            WidthRequest="300"
            HorizontalOptions="Center"
            Text="Machine Learning"
            Clicked="MachineLearning_Clicked">
            </Button>
</StackLayout>-->
```

7. Now let's add a grid, as follows, directly below
    the commented StackLayout XAML. GridLayout
    uses row definitions and column definitions to
    set up the format of the grid. Star (*) sizing means
    the row or column will use up all the available
    space proportionally. For example, if you have two
    columns that use * and *, each will be 50 percent
    of the available width. If you specify the first as *
    and the second as 2*, the first will be one-third of
    the width and the second will be two-thirds of the
    width available. A height or width set to Auto in
    the definitions will size automatically to the largest
    value in the row or column.

```
<Grid>
    <Grid.RowDefinitions>
        <RowDefinition Height="200"></RowDefinition>
        <RowDefinition Height="200"></RowDefinition>
    </Grid.RowDefinitions>
    <Grid.ColumnDefinitions>
        <ColumnDefinition Width="*">
        </ColumnDefinition>
        <ColumnDefinition Width="*">
        </ColumnDefinition>
    </Grid.ColumnDefinitions>
    <Button Grid.Row="0" Grid.Column="0"
    Margin="20,20"
            HorizontalOptions="Center"
            WidthRequest="300"
            Text="Microsoft Books"
            Clicked="MicrosoftBooks_Clicked">
            </Button>
```

```xml
<Button Grid.Row="0" Grid.Column="1"
Margin="20,20"
        HorizontalOptions="Center"
        WidthRequest="300"
       Text="Programming"
        Clicked="Programming_Clicked"></Button>
<Button Grid.Row="1" Grid.Column="0"
Margin="20,20"
        HorizontalOptions="Center"
        WidthRequest="300"
        Text="Mobile"
        Clicked="Mobile_Clicked"></Button>
<Button Grid.Row="1" Grid.Column="1"
Margin="20,20"
        HorizontalOptions="Center"
        WidthRequest="300"
       Text="Machine Learning"
        Clicked="MachineLearning_Clicked">
        </Button>
</Grid>
```

8. Run it, and you should see something like Figure 2-41.

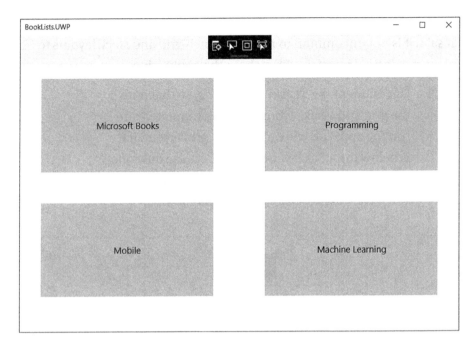

Figure 2-41.   *Using* GridLayout *for buttons*

Now let's look at how we use these in tablet and phone form factors.

Project 2-3: Dealing with Tablet and Phone Form Factors

Time Estimate

10 Minutes

In this task, you will use XAML and code behind to control your layout form factors for a tablet and a phone. ScrollView can be used in a phone form factor to represent the main page of an application. Many phone apps are typically used in portrait or landscape mode and have a single column which you must scroll down to see all the content. In a tablet form factor, the screen is wider, and a grid view on a main page can be used to maximize the real estate, because one can easily create columns. With that said, it is not uncommon to mix and match grid and stack layouts to achieve the desired interface throughout the application.

1. Uncomment the StackLayout code, so that both the grid and stack layouts are uncommented and run the app. You will only see the grid layout, if it is below the stack layout. This is because only one view can be returned for a page, and the last one in wins. We will fix that next. See Figure 2-42.

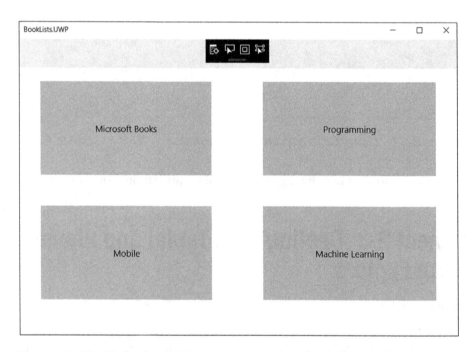

Figure 2-42. *Only the grid view shows when both layouts are uncommented. The last one in wins.*

2. **Try:** {What we would like to do is use the stack
    layout for the phone and the grid layout for the
    tablet. First, let's wrap both the grid and stack
    layout into one StackLayout view. Each section
    of the XAML can expand or contract using the –
    and + symbols on the left edge. Contract both grid
    and stack Layout sections, select both sections
    contracted, right-click and select Surround With...
    StackLayout.} See Figure 2-43.

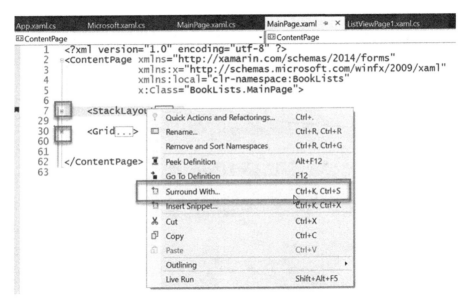

Figure 2-43. *Selecting Surround With...*

3. **Catch:** {Visual Studio may surround the code with
    a grid by default. Change it to a stack layout.} See
    Figure 2-44.

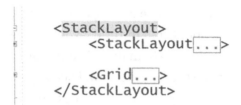

```
<StackLayout>
    <StackLayout...>

    <Grid...>
</StackLayout>
```

Figure 2-44. *StackLayout surrounds both StackLayout and Grid*

4. Run the app, and you will see that both sections are
    displayed on the page, which is almost where we
    want to be. See Figure 2-45.

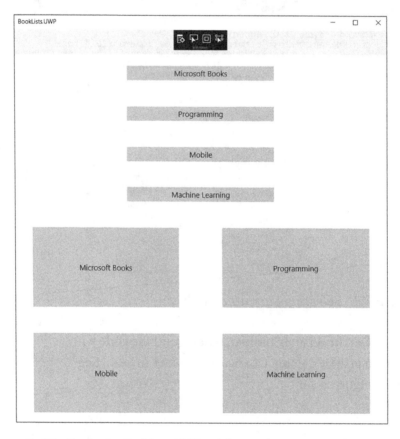

Figure 2-45. *Both the Grid and StackLayout views are displayed
when wrapped into a StackLayout*

5. Now let's make only the phone version view
    available on the phone and hide the tablet view,
    then make only the tablet view display on a tablet
    and hide the phone view. To do so, add a Name to
    the Tablet section called TabletView and the Phone
    section called PhoneView in the XAML, so we can
    refer to it in the code behind.

    ```
    <StackLayout>
        <StackLayout x:Name="PhoneView">

    ...

        <Grid x:Name="TabletView">
    </StackLayout>
    ```

6. After collapsing the buttons, it should look like
    Figure 2-46.

```xml
<?xml version="1.0" encoding="utf-8" ?>
<ContentPage xmlns="http://xamarin.com/schemas/2014/forms"
             xmlns:x="http://schemas.microsoft.com/winfx/2009/xaml"
             xmlns:local="clr-namespace:BookLists"
             x:Class="BookLists.MainPage">

    <StackLayout>
        <StackLayout x:Name="PhoneView">
            <Button Margin="20,20"...>
            <Button Margin="20,20"...>
            <Button Margin="20,20"...>
            <Button Margin="20,20"...>
        </StackLayout>


        <Grid x:Name="TabletView">
            <Grid.RowDefinitions>
                <RowDefinition Height="200"></RowDefinition>
                <RowDefinition Height="200"></RowDefinition>
            </Grid.RowDefinitions>
            <Grid.ColumnDefinitions>
                <ColumnDefinition Width="*"></ColumnDefinition>
                <ColumnDefinition Width="*"></ColumnDefinition>
            </Grid.ColumnDefinitions>
            <Button Grid.Row="0" Grid.Column="0" Margin="20,20"...>
            <Button Grid.Row="0" Grid.Column="1" Margin="20,20"...>
            <Button Grid.Row="1" Grid.Column="0" Margin="20,20"...>
            <Button Grid.Row="1" Grid.Column="1" Margin="20,20"...>
        </Grid>
    </StackLayout>

</ContentPage>
```

Figure 2-46. *MainPage.xaml should look like this*

7. Use Device.Idiom to detect if the device running
    this app is a phone in the code behind. In MainPage.
    xaml.cs, add this code in the constructor, right
    after InitializeComponent(). If it is a phone that is
    running the app, we are going to hide the tablet view
    and show the phone view and vice-versa.

```csharp
if (Device.Idiom == TargetIdiom.Phone)
{
    TabletView.IsVisible = false;
    PhoneView.IsVisible = true;
}
```

```
else
{
    TabletView.IsVisible = true;
    PhoneView.IsVisible = false;
}
```

8. Build the .NET Standard project and run the app in
    the desired phone and tablet emulators or attached
    devices. For example, right-click the Android project
    and select as startup, then select the 5" KitKat. Run.
    See Figures 2-47 and 2-48.

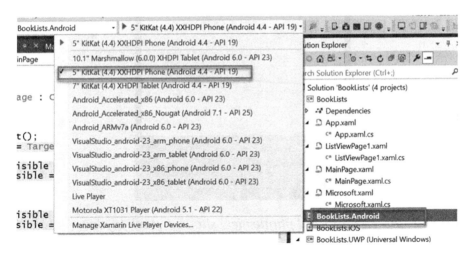

Figure 2-47. *Right-click Android project, set to startup, and then*
Select 5" KitKat from the drop-down menu

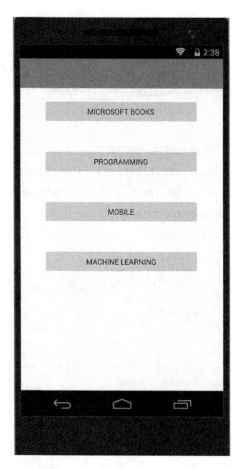

Figure 2-48. *The Android phone view shows a stack layout*

9. Then select UWP as the startup project and select
    Local Machine to run the tablet view on your laptop
    or desktop. See Figure 2-49.

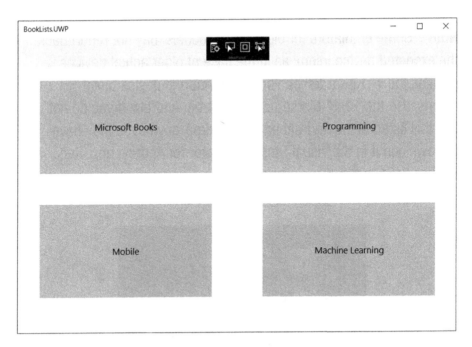

Figure 2-49. *Tablet view shows a grid layout*

10. Right-click Android project and set as startup. Select the 10.1" Marshmallow Tablet in Android from the emulator drop-down. See Figure 2-50.

Figure 2-50. *Selecting the 10.1" Marshmallow tablet*

Note   Some emulators for older tablet models may not report back
the expected device idiom, as in the case of older actual devices,
such as the 7" KitKat tablet. For testing Android device tablet
idioms, use the 10.1" Marshmallow tablet in Android. If you do not
see this listed in the Android emulators drop-down, you may have
to download it in the Visual Studio Emulator for Android app. See
Figures 2-51 and 2-52.

Figure 2-51. *Start the Visual Studio Emulator for Android app, if
needed, to download and install a 10.1" Marshmallow emulator*

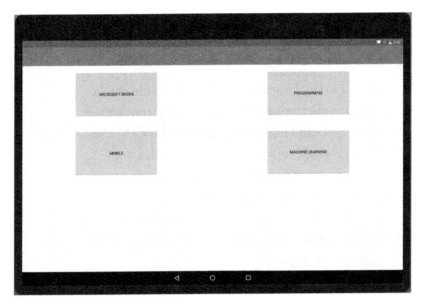

Figure 2-52. *Android tablet shows* Grid *view*

Project 2-4: Working with Images

Time Estimate

15 Minutes

1. In this project, you will learn how to access images locally, as embedded resources and Uniform Resource Identifiers (URIs). Also, you will use gesture recognizers to provide click event handlers. You could set the Button Image property to the image file name, but this really behaves differently across the platforms and causes many headaches. Plus, you cannot easily use aspect ratios on a button image. It is simpler to replace the buttons with image views. One problem, however, is that the image does not have a click event. So, we can use a gesture handler for this on the image, which will provide us a tapped event handler.

2. Let's replace the button text with images. But how? Images can be read locally from file or as embedded resources or can be downloaded from a URI.

3. To access local images from files, each file can be added to each application project and referenced from Xamarin Forms' shared .NET Standard code. To use a single image across all apps, the same file name must be used on every platform, and it should be a valid Android resource name (i.e., only lowercase letters, numerals, underscores, and periods are allowed. Also, the image cannot begin with a number).

4. For iOS, place images in the `Resources` folder with `Build Action: BundleResource`. Retina versions of the image should also be supplied—at two and three times the resolution, with @2x or @3x suffixes on the file name, before the file extension (e.g., `myimage@2x.png` and `myimage@3x.png`).

5. For Android, place images in the `Resources/drawable` directory with `Build Action: AndroidResource`. High- and low-DPI versions of an image can also be supplied (in appropriately named resources subdirectories, such as `drawable-ldpi`, `drawable-hdpi`, and `drawable-xhdpi`).

6. For Windows/UWP, place images in the application's root directory with `Build Action: Content`.

7. We are going to use embedded resources in our
    example. Create a new folder in the .NET Standard
    project called Images by right-clicking the project
    and selecting Add ➤ New Folder. See Figure 2-53.

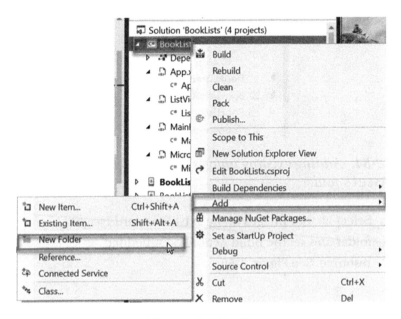

Figure 2-53. *Add New Folder and call it* Images

8. Add all four existing images to the Images folder in
    the Shared .NET Standard project from the book's
    /Assets folder or any set of four images that are of
    the dimensions 800 wide × 450 high. Right-click the
    Images folder and select Add ➤ Existing Item. See
    Figure 2-54.

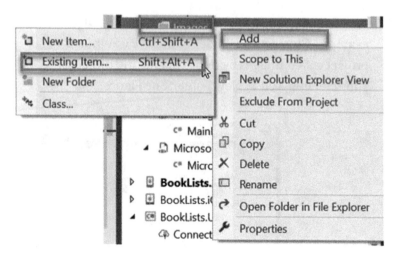

Figure 2-54. *Adding existing images to the project* Images *folder from* book /Assets *folder*

9. Select all four images in the .NET Standard Images folder and set the Build Action to Embedded resource. See Figure 2-55.

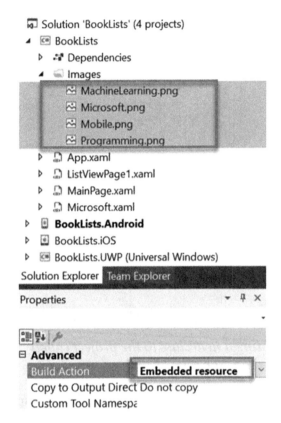

Figure 2-55. *Setting all four images to the Embedded resource Build Action*

10. Add a class to the .NET Standard project and call it ImageResourceExtension. See Figure 2-56.

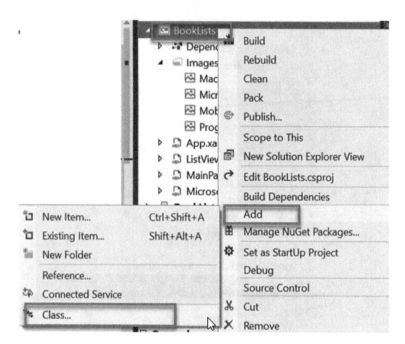

Figure 2-56. *Adding a new class to the project called*
ImageResourceExtension.cs

11. We must add a method to do a translation lookup for
    the XAML markup, by inheriting IMarkupExtension.
    Change the class to public and add the following
    code and using statements:

```
using System;
using Xamarin.Forms;
using Xamarin.Forms.Internals;
using Xamarin.Forms.Xaml;
using System.Reflection;

namespace BookLists
{
    // You exclude the 'Extension' suffix when using in
    // XAML markup
```

```
[Preserve(AllMembers = true)]
[ContentProperty("Source")]
public class ImageResourceExtension :
IMarkupExtension
{
    public string Source { get; set; }

    public object ProvideValue(IServiceProvider
    serviceProvider)
    {
        if (Source == null)
            return null;

        // Do your translation lookup here, using
        // whatever method you require
        var imageSource = ImageSource.
        FromResource(Source, Assembly.
        GetExecutingAssembly());

        return imageSource;
    }
}

}
```

12. Here is the new grid markup for the tablet version, using images, gesture recognizers, and labels. Verify your XAML and copy it, if necessary, to match for TabletView:

```
<Grid x:Name="TabletView"
VerticalOptions="FillAndExpand" Horizontal
Options="FillAndExpand">
    <Grid.RowDefinitions>
```

```
            <RowDefinition Height="40">
            </RowDefinition>
            <RowDefinition Height="*">
            </RowDefinition>
            <RowDefinition Height="Auto">
            </RowDefinition>
            <RowDefinition Height="*">
            </RowDefinition>
            <RowDefinition Height="Auto">
            </RowDefinition>
        </Grid.RowDefinitions>
        <Grid.ColumnDefinitions>
            <ColumnDefinition Width="*">
            </ColumnDefinition>
            <ColumnDefinition Width="*">
            </ColumnDefinition>
        </Grid.ColumnDefinitions>

        <Label Grid.Row="0" Grid.Column="0" Grid.
        ColumnSpan="2" VerticalOptions="Center"
        HorizontalOptions="Center"
        FontSize="Medium" FontAttributes="Bold"
        Text="Book List"></Label>
        <Image Grid.Row="1" Grid.
        Column="0" Aspect="AspectFill"
        Source="{local:ImageResource BookLists.
        Images.Microsoft.png}" >
            <Image.GestureRecognizers>
                <TapGestureRecognizer
                NumberOfTapsRequired="1"
                Tapped="MicrosoftBooks_Clicked"/>
            </Image.GestureRecognizers>
        </Image>
```

```
<Label Grid.Row="2" Grid.Column="0"
VerticalOptions="Center" FontSize="Small"
HorizontalTextAlignment="Center"
TextColor="Blue" Text="Microsoft"></Label>

<Image Grid.Row="3" Grid.Column="0"
Aspect="AspectFill"    Source="{local:
ImageResource BookLists.Images.Programming.
png}" >
    <Image.GestureRecognizers>
        <TapGestureRecognizer
        NumberOfTapsRequired="1"
        Tapped="Programming_Clicked"/>
    </Image.GestureRecognizers>
</Image>
<Label Grid.Row="4" Grid.Column="0"
VerticalOptions="Center" FontSize="Small"
HorizontalTextAlignment="Center"
TextColor="Blue"   Text="Programming">
</Label>
<Image   Grid.Row="1" Grid.Column="1"
Aspect="AspectFill"   Source="{local:Image
Resource BookLists.Images.Mobile.png}" >
    <Image.GestureRecognizers>
        <TapGestureRecognizer
        NumberOfTapsRequired="1"
        Tapped="Mobile_Clicked"/>
    </Image.GestureRecognizers>
</Image>
```

```
<Label Grid.Row="2" Grid.Column="1"
VerticalOptions="Center" FontSize="Small"
HorizontalTextAlignment="Center"
TextColor="Blue"  Text="Mobile"></Label>
<Image Grid.Row="3" Grid.
Column="1" Aspect="AspectFill"
Source="{local:ImageResource BookLists.
Images.MachineLearning.png}" >
    <Image.GestureRecognizers>
        <TapGestureRecognizer
        NumberOfTapsRequired="1"
        Tapped="MachineLearning_Clicked"/>
    </Image.GestureRecognizers>
</Image>
<Label Grid.Row="4" Grid.
Column="1" VerticalOptions="Center"
FontSize="Small"  HorizontalTextAlignment
="Center" TextColor="Blue" Text="Machine
Learning"></Label>

</Grid>
```

13. Run the app and click the Microsoft image on the home screen. You will see the mocked-up data ListView page. See Figure 2-57.

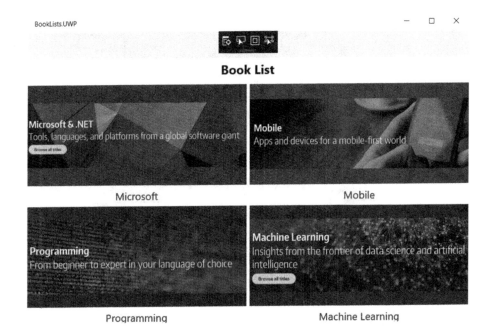

Figure 2-57. *Embedded images now show on* `MainPage` *and are clickable*

Project 2-5: Working with ListView

Time Estimate

10 Minutes

In this project, you will use the `ListViewPage` template with `TextCell` and `ViewCell` and the Caching strategy for recycling elements. You will use the `ListView` item, header, and footer templates.

1. Add a folder called `ViewModels` to the Booklists project. See Figure 2-58.

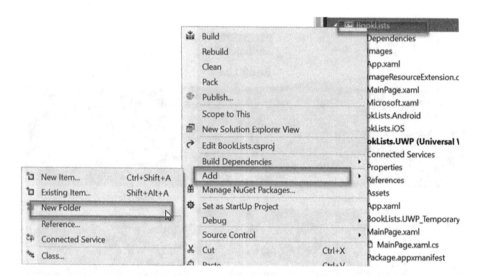

Figure 2-58. *Adding new folder called* `ViewModels`

2. Add exiting item from the /Assets folder for the book
   called **BookViewModel.cs**. This code contains a
   public class called `Item`, which has values for `Item`,
   `Detail`, and `URL`. It also has `ObservableCollection`,
   which has populated a few sample data records for
   Books. See Figure 2-59.

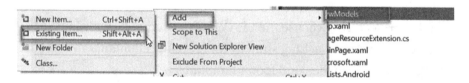

Figure 2-59. *Add existing item* `BookViewModel.cs` *to* `ViewModels`
folder

Here is the code in **BookViewModel.cs** that uses MVVM and Databinding. The MVVM pattern enforces a separation between three software layers. The underlying data is called the Model. The XAML user interface is called the View, and an intermediary that sits between the View and the Model is called the ViewModel. The View and the ViewModel are often connected through data bindings that are defined in the XAML file. BindingContext for View is usually an instance of ViewModel. Note the use of the INotifyPropertyChanged interface. The class doesn't invoke the PropertyChanged event unless the property has actually changed.

```
using System;
using System.Collections.Generic;
using System.Collections.ObjectModel;
using System.ComponentModel;
using System.Runtime.CompilerServices;
using System.Text;
using System.Threading.Tasks;
using System.Windows.Input;
using Xamarin.Forms;
using System.Linq;

namespace BookLists.ViewModels
{
    public class MicrosoftBooksViewModel :
    INotifyPropertyChanged
    {
```

```
public ObservableCollection<Item> Items { get; }

public ObservableCollection<Grouping<string,
Item>> ItemsGrouped { get; }

public MicrosoftBooksViewModel()
{
    Items = new ObservableCollection<Item>(new[]
    {
        new Item { Text = "Beginning Entity
        Framework Core 2.0",
            URL ="https://www.apress.com/us/
            book/9781484233740",
            Detail = "Use the valuable Entity
            Framework Core 2.0 tool in ASP.
            NET and the .NET Framework to
            eliminate the tedium around
            accessing databases and the data
            they contain. Entity Framework
            Core 2.0 greatly simplifies access
            to relational databases such as
            SQL Server that are commonly
            deployed in corporate settings.
            By eliminating tedious data
            access code that developers are
            otherwise forced to use, Entity
            Framework Core 2.0 enables you to
            work directly with the data in a
            database through domain-specific
            objects and methods." },

        new Item { Text = "Beginning Windows
        Mixed Reality Programming, For HoloLens
        and Mixed Reality Headsets",
```

```
            URL ="https://www.apress.com/us/
            book/9781484227688",
            Detail = "Develop applications
            and experiences for Microsoft's
            HoloLens and other Windows mixed
            reality devices. This easy-to-
            follow guide removes the mystery
            behind creating amazing augmented
            reality experiences. Mixed reality
            development tools and resources
            are provided. Beginning Windows
            Mixed Reality Programming clearly
            explains all the nuances of mixed
            reality software development.
            You'll learn how to create 3D
            objects and holograms, interact
            with holograms using voice commands
            and hand gestures, use spatial
            mapping and 3D spatial sound,
            build with Microsoft's HoloToolkit,
            create intuitive user interfaces,
            and make truly awe-inspiring mixed
            reality experiences. Start building
            the holographic future today!" },
new Item { Text = "Business in Real-
Time, Using Azure IoT and Cortana
Intelligence Suite Driving Your Digital
Transformation",
            URL ="https://www.apress.com/us/
            book/9781484226490",
```

Detail = "Learn how today's
businesses can transform themselves
by leveraging real-time data
and advanced machine learning
analytics. This book provides
prescriptive guidance for architects
and developers on the design and
development of modern Internet of
Things(IoT) and Advanced Analytics
solutions.In addition, Business
in Real - Time Using Azure IoT and
Cortana Intelligence Suite offers
patterns and practices for those
looking to engage their customers
and partners through Software
-as- a - Service solutions that
work on any device. Whether you're
working in Health & Life Sciences,
Manufacturing, Retail, Smart
Cities and Buildings or Process
Control, there exists a common
platform from which you can create
your targeted vertical solutions.
Business in Real-Time Using Azure
IoT and Cortana Intelligence Suite
uses a reference architecture as
a road map. Building on Azure's
PaaS services, you'll see how a
solution architecture unfolds that
demonstrates a complete end - to -
end IoT and Advanced Analytics
scenario." },

```
new Item { Text = "Cyber Security on
Azure, An IT Professional's Guide to
Microsoft Azure Security Center",
        URL ="https://www.apress.com/us/
        book/9781484227398",
        Detail = "Prevent destructive
        attacks to your Azure public
        cloud infrastructure, remove
        vulnerabilities, and instantly
        report cloud security readiness.
        This book provides comprehensive
        guidance from a security insider's
        perspective. Cyber Security on
        Azure explains how this 'security
        as a service' (SECaaS) business
        solution can help you better manage
        security risk and enable data
        security control using encryption
        options such as Advanced Encryption
        Standard(AES) cryptography.Discover
        best practices to support network
        security groups, web application
        firewalls, and database auditing
        for threat protection. Configure
        custom security notifications of
        potential cyberattack vectors
        to prevent unauthorized access
        by hackers, hacktivists, and
        industrial spies." },
new Item { Text = "Essential Angular
for ASP.NET Core MVC",
```

```
                        URL ="https://www.apress.com/us/
                        book/9781484229156",
                        Detail = "Angular 5 and .NET Core
                        2 updates for this book are now
                        available. Follow the Download
                        Source Code link for this book
                        on the Apress website. Discover
                        Angular, the leading client-side
                        web framework, from the point
                        of view of an ASP.NET Core MVC
                        developer. Best-selling author
                        Adam Freeman brings these two key
                        technologies together and explains
                        how to use ASP.NET Core MVC to
                        provide back-end services for
                        Angular applications. This fast -
                        paced, practical guide starts from
                        the nuts and bolt and gives you
                        the knowledge you need to combine
                        Angular(from version 2.0 up) and
                        ASP.NET Core MVC in your projects.
                        " },

            });

    var sorted = from item in Items
                        orderby item.Text
                        group item by item.Text[0].
                        ToString() into itemGroup
                        select new Grouping<string,
                        Item>(itemGroup.Key,
                        itemGroup);
```

```
    ItemsGrouped = new ObservableCollection
    <Grouping<string, Item>>(sorted);

    RefreshDataCommand = new Command(
        async () => await RefreshData());
}

public ICommand RefreshDataCommand { get; }

async Task RefreshData()
{
    IsBusy = true;
    //Load Data Here
    await Task.Delay(2000);

    IsBusy = false;
}

bool busy;
public bool IsBusy
{
    get { return busy; }
    set
    {
        busy = value;
        OnPropertyChanged();
        ((Command)RefreshDataCommand).
        ChangeCanExecute();
    }
}
```

```csharp
public event PropertyChangedEventHandler
PropertyChanged;
void OnPropertyChanged([CallerMemberName]string
propertyName = "") =>
    PropertyChanged?.Invoke(this, new Property
    ChangedEventArgs(propertyName));

public class Item
{
    public string Text { get; set; }
    public string Detail { get; set; }
    public string URL { get; set; }
    public override string ToString() => URL;
}

public class Grouping<K, T> :
ObservableCollection<T>
{
    public K Key { get; private set; }

    public Grouping(K key, IEnumerable<T> items)
    {
        Key = key;
        foreach (var item in items)
            this.Items.Add(item);
    }
}
    }
}
```

3. Open the code behind page Microsoft.xaml.cs.

4. Add this line under InitializeComponent():

```csharp
BindingContext = new MicrosoftBooksViewModel();
```

5. You will also need to add this using statement:

    using BookLists.ViewModels;

6. Comment out the following lines:

    ```
    //          Items = new ObservableCollection<string>
    //          {
    //              "Item 1",
    //              "Item 2",
    //              "Item 3",
    //              "Item 4",
    //              "Item 5"
    //          };

    //MyListView.ItemsSource = Items;
    ```

7. Comment out the Handle_ItemTapped event code
    and add the **Handle_ItemSelected** event handler
    with this code:

    ```
    void Handle_ItemSelected(object sender,
    SelectedItemChangedEventArgs e)
       {
           if (e.SelectedItem == null)
               return;

       // await DisplayAlert("Selected",
       // e.SelectedItem.ToString(), "OK");
       //    navigate to the URL with the native
       // browser

       Device.OpenUri(new Uri(e.SelectedItem.
       ToString()));
    ```

```
                //Deselect Item
            ((ListView)sender).SelectedItem = null;
            }
        }
```

8. Your Microsoft.xaml.cs file should now look like this:

```
using BookLists.ViewModels;
using System;
using Xamarin.Forms;
using Xamarin.Forms.Xaml;

namespace BookLists
{
    [XamlCompilation(XamlCompilationOptions.Compile)]
    public partial class Microsoft : ContentPage
    {
        public Microsoft()
        {
            InitializeComponent();
            BindingContext = new
            MicrosoftBooksViewModel();
                //          Items = new
                // ObservableCollection<string>
                //          {
                //              "Item 1",
                //              "Item 2",
                //              "Item 3",
                //              "Item 4",
                //              "Item 5"
                //          };

                //MyListView.ItemsSource = Items;
        }
```

```
void Handle_ItemSelected(object sender,
SelectedItemChangedEventArgs e)
    {
        if (e.SelectedItem == null)
            return;
        // await DisplayAlert("Selected",
        // e.SelectedItem.ToString(), "OK");
        // navigate to the URL with the native browser
        Device.OpenUri(new Uri(e.SelectedItem.
        ToString()));
    }
}
}
```

9. Open `Microsoft.xaml` and replace the `ListView`
with the following XAML (note that it uses a custom
`ViewCell` with a Header, `ItemTemplate`, and
Footer).

```
<ListView x:Name="BookListView"
ItemsSource="{Binding ItemsGrouped}"
        ItemSelected="Handle_ItemSelected"
        HasUnevenRows="true"
        GroupShortNameBinding="{Binding Key}"
        IsGroupingEnabled="true"
        GroupDisplayBinding="{Binding Key}"
        IsPullToRefreshEnabled="true"
        CachingStrategy="RecycleElement"
        IsRefreshing="{Binding IsBusy, Mode=OneWay}"
        RefreshCommand="{Binding RefreshDataCommand}"
        >
```

```
                    <!--Built in Cells-->
      <!--<ListView.ItemTemplate>
          <DataTemplate>
              <TextCell Text="{Binding .}" />
          </DataTemplate>
      </ListView.ItemTemplate>-->

      <!--Custom View Cells-->
          <ListView.Header>
              <StackLayout Padding="10"
                      Orientation="Horizontal"
                      HorizontalOptions="FillAndExpand"
                      BackgroundColor="#dadada">
                <Label Text="Microsoft and .NET Books"
              HorizontalTextAlignment="Center"
              HorizontalOptions="FillAndExpand"
              TextColor="Black"
              FontAttributes="Bold"/>
              </StackLayout>
          </ListView.Header>
          <ListView.ItemTemplate>
      <DataTemplate>
        <ViewCell>
          <StackLayout>
            <Label Text="{Binding Text}"
                    Style="{DynamicResource
                    ListItemTextStyle}"
                    FontAttributes="Bold"/>
```

```
        <Label Text="{Binding Detail}"
                Style="{DynamicResource
                ListItemDetailTextStyle}"/>
          </StackLayout>
        </ViewCell>
      </DataTemplate>
    </ListView.ItemTemplate>
    <ListView.Footer>
        <StackLayout Padding="10"
                Orientation="Horizontal"
                HorizontalOptions="FillAndExpand"
                BackgroundColor="#dadada">
            <Label Text="Visit www.apress.com"
          HorizontalTextAlignment="Center"
          HorizontalOptions="FillAndExpand"
          TextColor="Black"
          FontAttributes="Bold"/>
        </StackLayout>
    </ListView.Footer>
</ListView>
```

10. Run the app and click the Microsoft image on the
    home screen. You will see something like Figures 2-60
    and 2-61.

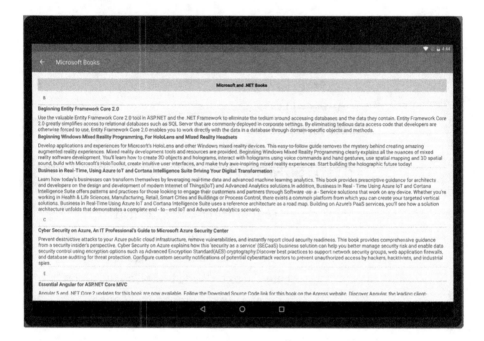

Figure 2-60. `ListView` *on Android tablet with header, groupings, and footer*

Figure 2-61. *ListView on UWP with header, groupings, and footer*

11. **Try:** Click an item in the list, and it will open an external browser to the desired URL. See Figure 2-62.

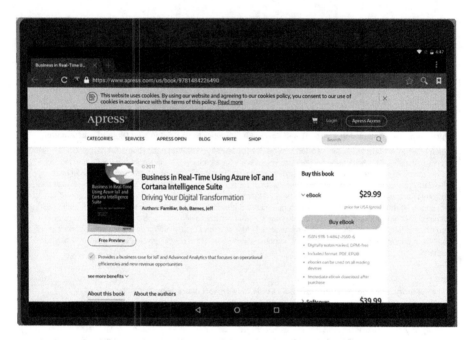

Figure 2-62. *URL displayed in native browser on device*

12. **Catch:** The UWP `ListView` may have an error only on clicking and getting the correct selected item in the list when using the `ListView` group optionally. (Android and iOS should work.) This has been fixed with version 2.5.0.280555 of Xamarin Forms. Right-click the solution and select Manage NuGet Packages to verify that you have a minimum version of 2.5.0.280555. If not, check the updates panel to install. See Figure 2-63.

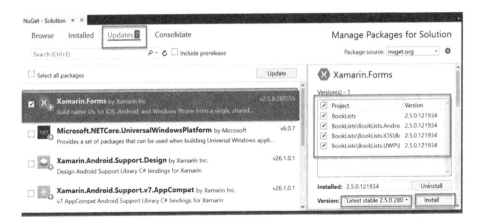

Figure 2-63. *Verifying that the installed Xamarin Forms NuGet package is a minimum version of 2.5.0.280555. If not, select the Updates tab and intall it.*

13.   One important property on the ListView,
       especially for Android apps, is **CachingStrategy**.
       Note that the ListView template page has it set
       to "RecycleElement". This is not the default on
       ListView for backward compatibility and must
       be specified to take effect. This option provides
       significant performance improvements, particularly
       in Android. RetainElement is the default, and
       it's not optimal, especially when dealing with
       large lists. However, the UWP platform ignores
       ListViewCachingStrategy.RetainElement,
       because it always uses caching to improve
       performance. See Figure 2-64.

```
<ListView x:Name="BookListView" ItemsSource="{Binding ItemsGrouped}"
        ItemSelected="Handle_ItemSelected"
        HasUnevenRows="true"
        GroupShortNameBinding="{Binding Key}"
        IsGroupingEnabled="true"
        GroupDisplayBinding="{Binding Key}"
        IsPullToRefreshEnabled="true"
        CachingStrategy="RecycleElement"
        IsRefreshing="{Binding IsBusy, Mode=OneWay}"
        RefreshCommand="{Binding RefreshDataCommand}"
        >
```

Figure 2-64. Specify `CachingStrategy="RecycleElement"`, *as it is not a default*

Summary

In this chapter, you created a new Xamarin Forms application. The application can run on Android, UWP, and, optionally, iOS, if connected with a Mac server. As this is a cross platform app, you can use any mix of the platform projects, depending on your development environment (Mac or Windows). You enhanced the app with StackLayout and GridLayout to have a main navigation page and used device form factors for phones and tablets, with device specific logic. The main page uses embedded resource images. A ListView page template was added with a customization for selection event handlers and content. Next up? You get to learn Azure. Let the games begin!

CHAPTER 3

Introduction to Azure: A Developer's Perspective

From a developer's perspective, Azure is about getting your apps to market faster. Azure is a worldwide network of managed service centers that facilitate building, testing, and deploying apps. You can build applications using any dev tool or language, including Node.js, Java, and .NET, with best-of-class tools in Visual Studio and Visual Studio Code, on either your PC or Mac. But wait, there's more! You have a choice of more than 100 services to provide your users richer experiences, whether through responsive web apps, native mobile apps, or new features, such as mixed reality and bots. Azure provides an end-to-end management experience by using your choice of management tools, including Power Shell, BASH, the Azure portal, or REST APIs. We will look at how Azure can provide cross-device experiences with support for all major mobile platforms.

This chapter will guide you through taking your first steps in working with Azure and provide a tour of the portal. You will see how to get a free $200 30-day account, as well as several per-month usage credit options. This benefit is subject to change. The "free credit" may just do the job of getting your feet wet in learning Azure, and the recurring monthly credits may just do the job, period.

© Russell Fustino 2018
R. Fustino, *Azure and Xamarin Forms*, https://doi.org/10.1007/978-1-4842-3561-4_3

I will cover the following in this chapter:

- Monitoring your billing and usage

- Creating a virtual machine

- ASP.NET web services

- Deploying from GitHub and Visual Studio

- Deployment models and resource groups

- Azure command-line interface (CLI)

- Creating SQL (Structured Query Language) database and scalability

- How to grow your solutions and find useful resources on `azure.microsoft.com` related to support and architectures

- How to delete learning resources

Time Estimate

120 Minutes

Free Azure Accounts and Credits

There are various offers available for free credits on Azure usage, specifically for developers. In this section, we will look at how to use Azure for free initially and how to get recurring free credits.

Signing up for a free account is a great way to explore Azure, without any commitment. As part of the free account, you are getting an Azure subscription that lets you create, manage, and scale resources and a $200 credit to spend on Azure services for 30 days. You can use those credits to try out any combination of Azure services.

If you do not have a Microsoft account or have used up your free credits in the past, create a new account at `https://signup.live.com` and then join the Visual Studio Dev Essentials program with that account at `www.visualstudio.com/dev-essentials/` and claim some free stuff. See Figure 3-1.

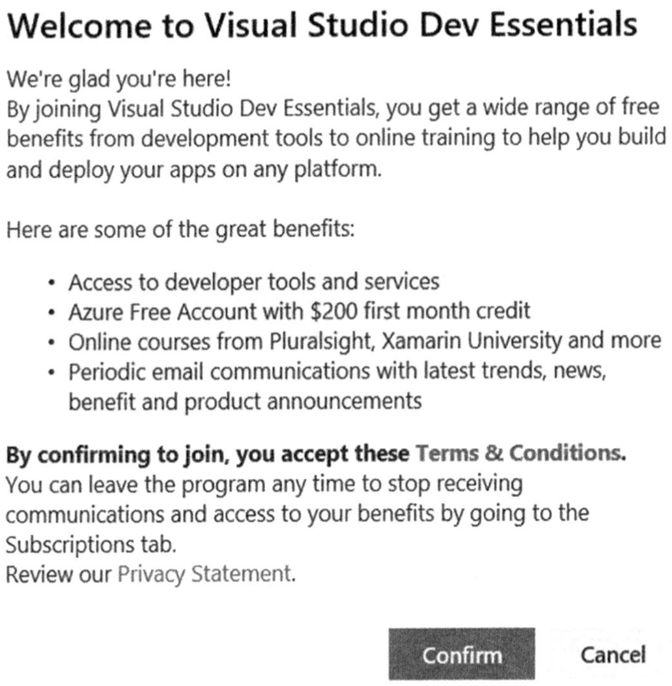

Welcome to Visual Studio Dev Essentials

We're glad you're here!
By joining Visual Studio Dev Essentials, you get a wide range of free benefits from development tools to online training to help you build and deploy your apps on any platform.

Here are some of the great benefits:

- Access to developer tools and services
- Azure Free Account with $200 first month credit
- Online courses from Pluralsight, Xamarin University and more
- Periodic email communications with latest trends, news, benefit and product announcements

By confirming to join, you accept these Terms & Conditions.
You can leave the program any time to stop receiving communications and access to your benefits by going to the Subscriptions tab.
Review our Privacy Statement.

Confirm   Cancel

Figure 3-1. Visual Studio Dev Essentials benefits

The Free Visual Studio Dev Essentials account is completely free, and you won't be charged for anything during the term of usage. Even when your 30 days are over, Microsoft will not automatically convert your account to a paid account and start charging you. The only reason Microsoft asks for a credit card is to verify your identity and prevent fraud.

You can always see the number of remaining days of your trial and remaining credit when you log on to the Azure portal, so you always know where you stand. In case you use all your credits, or your 30-day trial is over, Microsoft will notify you, so you can decide if you want to transition to a pay-as-you-go subscription. If you do, great. You start paying for the services you want to use. If not, don't worry, you won't be billed for anything, but you will no longer be able to access previous services.

I hope you enjoy your free accounts and make good use of your $200 credit. In addition to the Azure $200 credit, there are many more benefits available on the Azure site, including downloads for Visual Studio Community, Visual Studio for the Mac, and more, so be sure to look at these great developer benefits.

1. To start, click the Azure Activate offer for a free account and a $200 credit. See Figure 3-2.

Figure 3-2. *Activating the free Azure credit*

2. You will then be prompted for personal information. Fill out the About You, Identity verification by phone, Identity verification by card, and Agreement sections. See Figure 3-3.

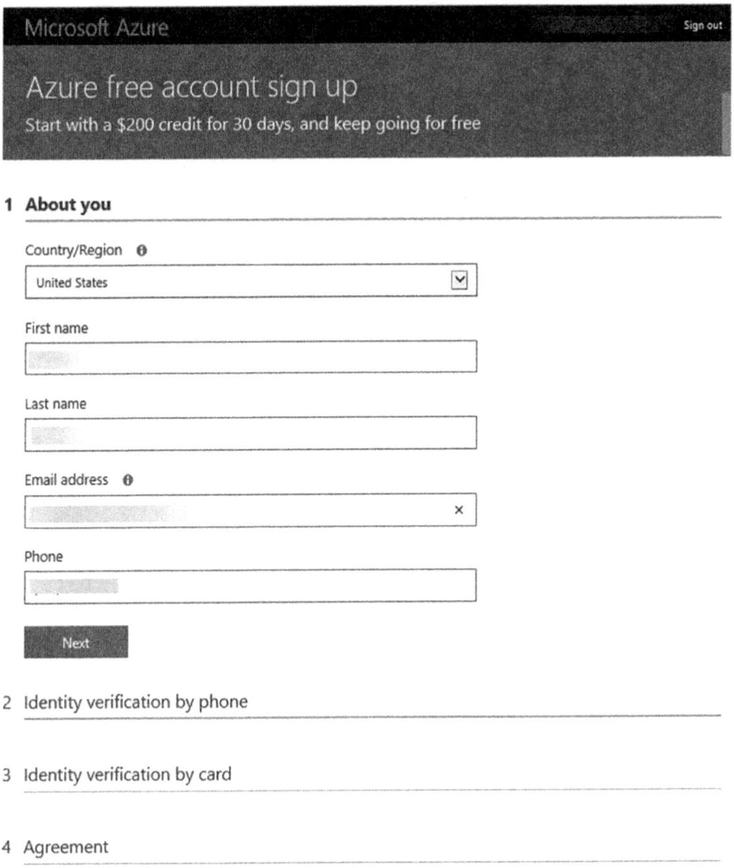

Microsoft Azure   Sign out

Azure free account sign up
Start with a $200 credit for 30 days, and keep going for free

1 About you

Country/Region ❶

United States

First name

Last name

Email address ❶

×

Phone

Next

2 Identity verification by phone

3 Identity verification by card

4 Agreement

Figure 3-3. *Azure free account signup*

3. You will then be directed to the Azure portal
    welcome page, with usage questions, resources,
    tutorials, and webcasts. See Figure 3-4.

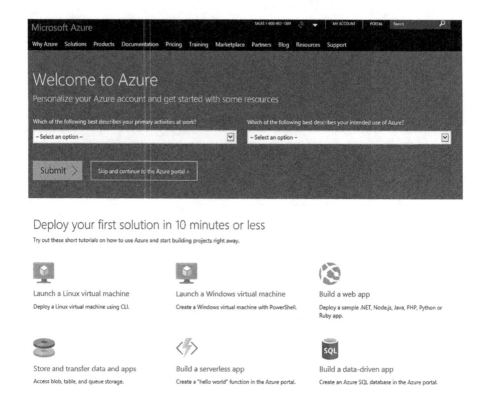

Figure 3-4. *Azure welcome page*

4. Once the questions have been answered, you can
    bookmark this page, to return to it, and then click
    Continue to Azure portal. See Figures 3-5 and 3-6.

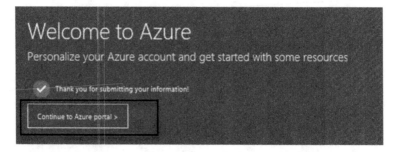

Figure 3-5. *Continue to portal*

94

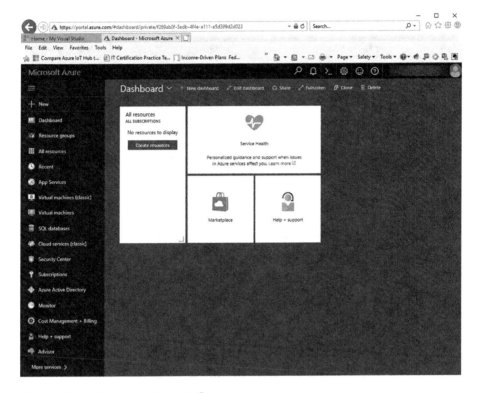

Figure 3-6. `https://portal.azure.com`

5. Also, if you have a Visual Studio Professional
    Subscription, you can receive a $50 monthly credit,
    or, with a Visual Studio Enterprise Subscription, a
    $150 monthly credit. See Figure 3-7.

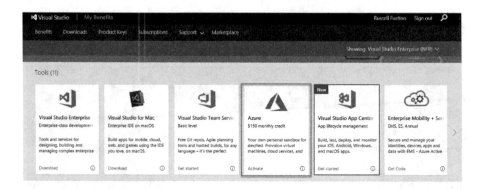

Figure 3-7. $150 monthly Azure credit for Visual Studio Enterprise

6. If you are a Microsoft Partner, you can receive a
    $100 monthly Azure credit through an Action Pack
    subscription purchase. For details, see `https://`
    `partner.microsoft.com/en-us/membership/`
    `action-pack`.

7. Through the Microsoft startup program BizSpark,
    you can receive a $150-per-month Azure credit
    for up to five developers. For details, see `https://`
    `bizspark.microsoft.com/`.

Once you have an Azure subscription, you can start creating and
managing resources in Azure. The easiest way to start doing that is through
the Azure portal.

Azure Portal

To get to the Azure portal, you can either go to `azure.microsoft.com` and
click the portal link at the top of the page or simply navigate to `portal.`
`azure.com`.

After you log on to the portal, you will see the main dashboard. You will see your recent resources, some health information, and some Get Started content. See Figure 3-8.

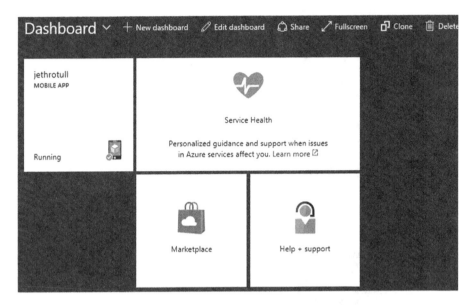

Figure 3-8. *The Azure portal dashboard shows resources, health information, and help and support, which includes getting started information*

On the left, there is a navigation pane that helps you browse your resources by type. You can see your virtual machines, databases, or go back and see all the resources. The list of resources on this navigator includes only your favorites, and if you click More services, you can see the full list. You can scroll through the list and mark additional resource types as favorites. See Figure 3-9.

Figure 3-9. *Azure navigation pane. Click More services to see all choices. Mark your favorites by clicking a star.*

Use the Search box to filter. Type in a search for SQL. See Figure 3-10.

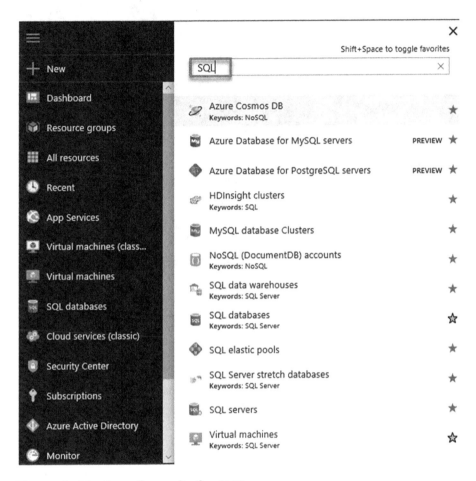

Figure 3-10.   *Search results for SQL*

On the top bar, there is a settings area that lets you pick different themes and change the portal's language. See Figure 3-11.

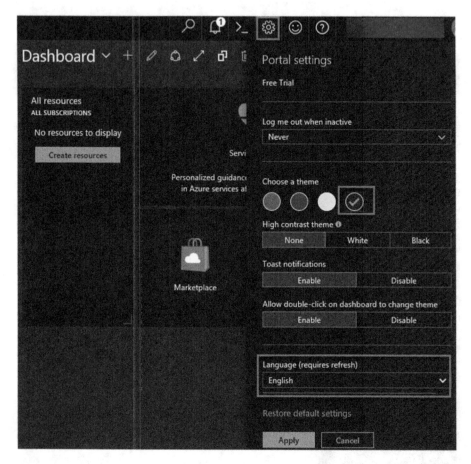

Figure 3-11. *Azure portal settings for theme and language*

From the Help button, you can submit support requests and see all the keyboard shortcuts, which become very useful. For example, you can always click "?" to show and hide the keyboard shortcuts page and press the G and slash to get to the search bar and search for resources. See Figures 3-12 and 3-13.

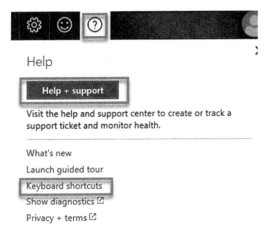

Figure 3-12. *Azure portal Help menu*

Figure 3-13. *Azure portal keyboard shortcuts. Use G+/ to search resources.*

Using the smiley face at the top, you can contact support and provide feedback about your experience with the portal. The portal team listens carefully and improves the experience, based on customer feedback. See Figure 3-14.

Figure 3-14. *Azure portal feedback*

You also have a notification icon that updates you on any changes since your last login and shows you your remaining credit. See Figure 3-15.

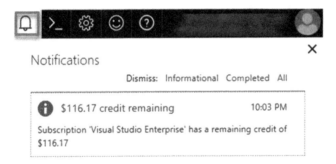

Figure 3-15. *Azure notifications with remaining credits*

Billing and Usage

If you want to drill deeper into your billing information, to see how you are spending your credits, you can go to the subscription section through the navigator on the left. On the subscription information page, you can see all your subscriptions, your burn rate, how much you spend per resource, and, if you click on invoices, your most recent invoices for the subscription. So, you can get good visibility on where you are spending your money or trial credits. See Figures 3-16 and 3-17.

Figure 3-16. *Subscription information*

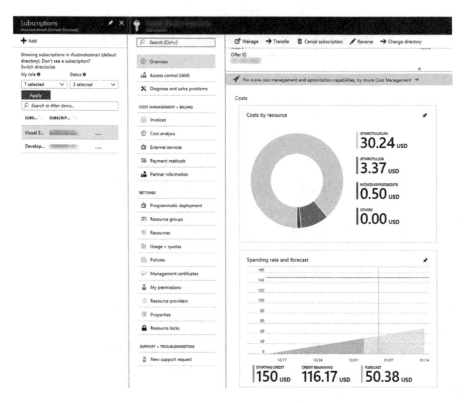

Figure 3-17. *Drilling down into resources used and burn rate*

Now that we have one of the biggest fears, on measuring costs in Azure, under control, let's move on to one of the biggest reasons for using Azure: the Marketplace.

Marketplace

The Marketplace is the top destination for all your developer needs, optimized and certified to run on Azure. It is a great place to find the solutions you need, in a rich catalog of thousands of end-to-end solutions and products. For example, later in the chapter, I will show how to provision a virtual machine with Visual Studio already installed from the

Marketplace. This provisioning takes only about 10 minutes. Compare that if you were to install Visual Studio alone on a standalone machine. It could take an hour or two. You can also leverage free trials from independent software vendors (ISVs), to deploy and use the software in your subscription. Happy surfing in the Marketplace. Let's get started.

If you press *G* and *N* on your keyboard or click the +New link, you can start creating resources in Azure. You can scroll through the categories and select which item you would like to create. For example, you can create Windows or Linux virtual machines from the Compute category, create web apps from the Web and Mobile category, or create new relational or NoSQL databases from the Databases category. See Figure 3-18.

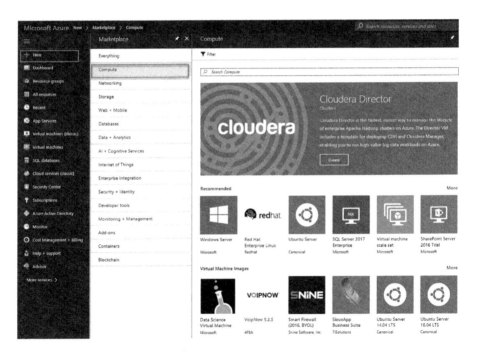

Figure 3-18. *Click +New to create a resource*

You can also open the Marketplace and see a comprehensive list of thousands of items, not just from Microsoft, but from other vendors as well. These items can be provisioned or purchased. You can search everything (search for Hadoop), or explore by categories. Currently, the Marketplace has about 3,500 items, from numerous vendors, to choose from. See Figure 3-19.

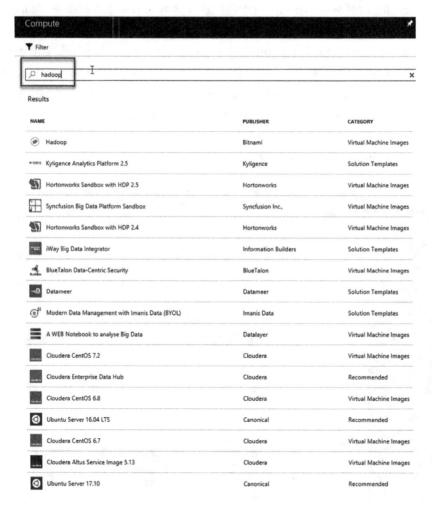

Figure 3-19. *Search results in Marketplace for Hadoop*

Now that you have a handle on the overview of Marketplace, let's start using it to provision a virtual machine.

Windows Virtual Machines

One of the earliest uses of Azure was to create virtual machines (VMs). Why? VMs are the root of any company considering to "lift and shift" data-center operations to the cloud. For example, instead of running servers on-site, they can be run from the cloud. Benefits include lower costs for operation and support and ease of scalability.

Now let's create a virtual machine in the cloud. You can either search for the virtual machine image you want or browse through what is available in the Marketplace. Azure has a huge gallery of virtual machine images to pick from. There are preconfigured VMs for such things as SQL and Drupal and complete multi-VM solution templates for larger systems, such as SharePoint or WebSphere.

If you want to create a Linux VM, you can search for popular images like Ubuntu, Red Hat, or more, but in this section, you will create a developer VM Windows 10 machine with Visual Studio installed. We have lots of different versions to choose from, so, first, search on Visual Studio. See Figure 3-20.

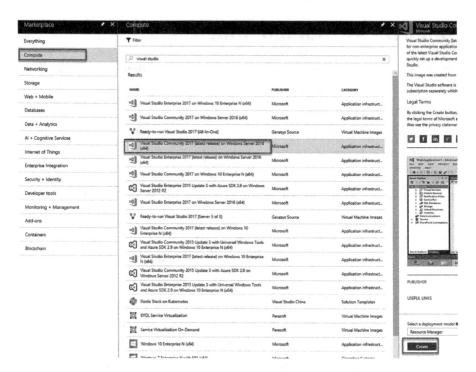

Figure 3-20. *Search results in Visual Studio. Select VS Community 2017 (latest release) on Windows Server 2016.*

If you have an MSDN subscription, you can select the same for Windows 10 for UWP dev in this book. You will not be able to do UWP dev on a Windows Server machine.

1. After selecting VS Community 2017 (latest release) on Windows Server 2016, click Create virtual machine. If you have a MSDB subscription, you can select the Windows 10 version to create the UWP apps in this book. At the time of writing, Windows 10 is not available with the free $200 credit offer.

2. Enter "Demo@pass123" as the password. Choose
    a location near you (use this location for the
    remainder of this chapter) and the remainder of the
    basics, as shown in Figure 3-21. In the Basics settings,
    we create a Resource group that is a container of
    multiple resources used for an app. In this case,
    because we are creating a single VM, we create a
    new resource group, using the name "demorg." If
    we group resources under the same name, we can
    easily delete them, for example, altogether, by simply
    deleting the resource group. Click OK.

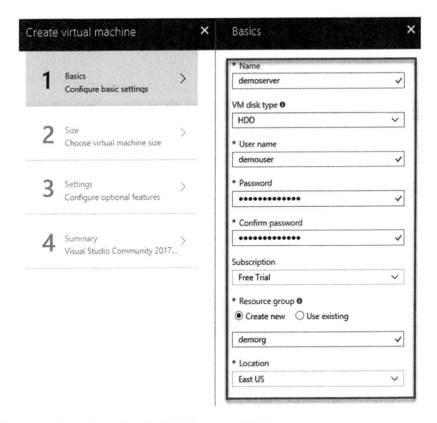

Figure 3-21. *Enter basic info for your VM*

3. Under Choose a size, click View all, then click on one of the least expensive options, as you will be deleting this at the end of this chapter. Select A1 Basic, which will work for this chapter. This machine will be very sluggish, and it will be a throwaway, as we are only creating it to demonstrate how to use it. See Figures 3-22 and 3-23.

Figure 3-22. *Select View all*

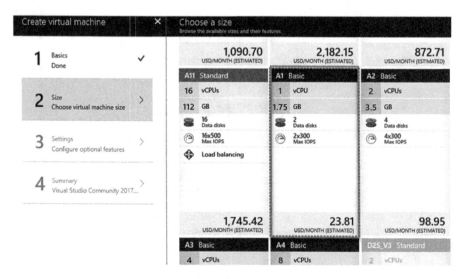

Figure 3-23. *Pick A1 Basic*

4. Keep all the defaults on the Settings blade and click OK on the Summary blade. See Figure 3-24.

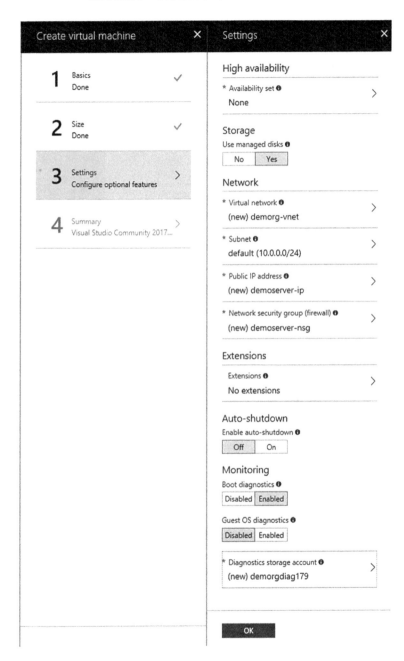

Figure 3-24. *Keep the settings defaults*

5. The deployment will take about 15–20 minutes to complete. You will receive a notification when it finishes. See Figures 3-25 and 3-26.

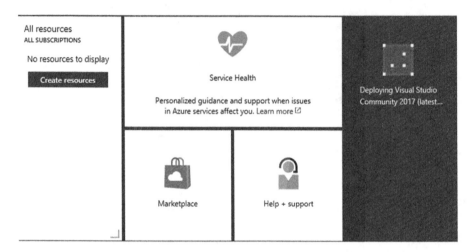

Figure 3-25. *Deploying Visual Studio VM*

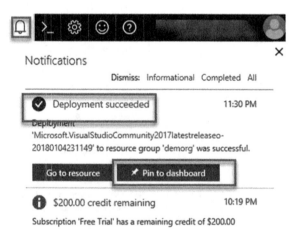

Figure 3-26. *Notification that deployment succeeded*

6. While this is deploying, let's look at a few resources. Open a new tab in your browser and navigate to the Azure site and the regions map at `http://azure.microsoft.com/regions`. Azure has 50 regions available in 140 countries. You can visit the Azure regions page to see a map of all the regions and decide on the best location to deploy to. Azure offers scale needed to bring applications closer to users around the globe, providing data residency and resiliency options for end customers. See Figure 3-27.

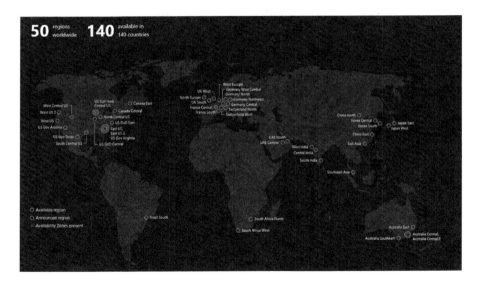

Figure 3-27. *Azure regions map*

7. As for VM sizes, you should choose the right VM for your workload, based on the number of cores, the memory, disk drive size, and price. Azure will give you recommendations based on popular sizes, but you can also click View all to see more options.

8. Once the deployment completes, you can pin it, so
    that it appears on your dashboard, or you can get to
    it from the Virtual Machines list on the left pane, or
    you can search for it using the search bar.

9. On the details page, you can monitor and manage this
    virtual machine. You can look at the CPU, disk, and
    network usage; go to the activity log; and diagnose
    problems. You can add additional disks or change
    this virtual machine size even after it's been created.
    Because this is a Windows virtual machine, click
    connect, download a RDP file that you can then open,
    and we're now going to remote desktop into this
    virtual machine running in Azure. See Figure 3-28.

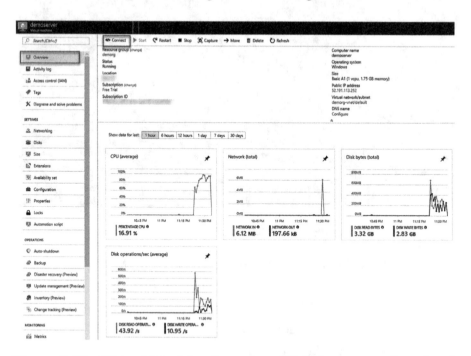

Figure 3-28. *Virtual Machine Overview. Click Connect to download
an RDP file.*

10. When prompted for credentials, click More choices, to enter the demouser credentials we set up. See Figures 3-29 and 3-30.

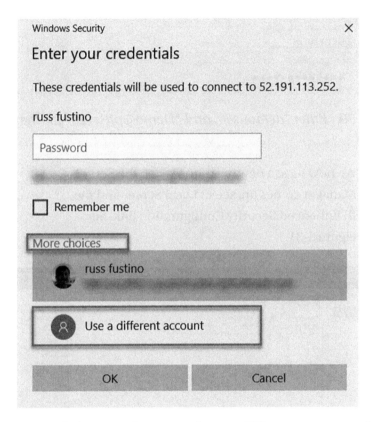

Figure 3-29. *Click More choices and use a different account when prompted for credentials*

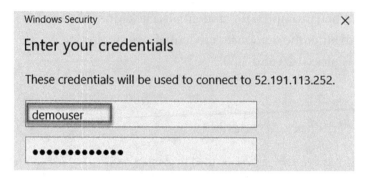

Figure 3-30. Enter "demouser" and "Demo@pass123" for the password

11. We now have a new machine! When the Server Manager comes up, select Local Server and the IE Enhanced Security Configuration link. See Figure 3-31.

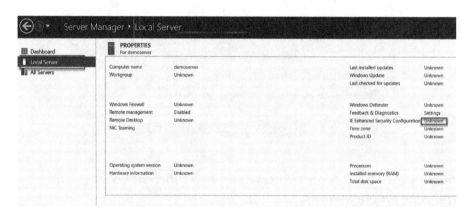

Figure 3-31. In Server Manager, click Local Server and IE Enhanced Security Configuration

12. Set the Internet Explorer Enhanced Security Configuration to off (Figure 3-32), or you will be nagged every time you navigate to a site not already on the list. Of course, this all depends on your security needs.

Figure 3-32. *Set the enhanced security configuration to off*

Creating virtual machines in the Azure portal is very easy, and in just a few minutes, we were able to create resources in the cloud, including an install of Visual Studio!

One note about Xamarin and Azure VMs: At the moment, it is very difficult to use this combination. First, on a Windows Server VM, you cannot create a UWP app on that platform in Visual Studio. You can create a Windows 10 VM but requires an MSDN subscription to do this, as you cannot create a Windows 10 VM with the free 30-day trial subscription. Even if you have an Azure Windows 10 VM with which you can create UWP apps, the emulators do not run in the VM, and there goes Android and iOS dev. You could look into Genymotion for the Android emulator, however, and that may work. iOS must connect on your network to a Mac, and the VM is not on your network; it is on Azure's. So, at this point, I recommend using VS on the metal for Xamarin development and not in an Azure VM.

When we created our virtual machine, I mentioned something called resource groups. I want to give you more context about that in the next section.

Deployment Models and Resource Groups

If you click the More services button again and go through the types of resources you can manage in the portal, you'll see that there are two kinds of virtual machines. One says "Virtual Machines," and the other says "Classic." Here is why:

Azure has two deployment models. The classic deployment model is the original model from the first days of Azure. This model is centered on the individual service, and every API call is made to make a single operation on a single resource, for example, create a web site, stop a web site.

This model works well. But, as cloud solutions are becoming more complex and composed of multiple services, it is becoming difficult to deploy a solution by configuring each service independently.

The more recent deployment model, which is now the standard model in the Azure portal, is called ARM, which stands for *Azure Resource Management.* This model looks at the world through resource groups that let you group multiple resources and create or manage them together. As an example, if I look at my virtual machines, I can click on one of them and see whether my VM belongs to a resource group. Drilling into that resource group shows me that it includes a bunch of resources: the virtual machine, the network interface, the public IP address, and storage. All those items were created as a single operation when I created the virtual machine. And, if I ever want to remove my virtual machine, I can simply remove this resource group, and all my related resources will be deleted as well.

I can also see the cost of each of the resources in this group, but, more important, I can get the code or template that can be used to re-create this resource group. Resource groups can be represented using a template, which is a JSON file that defines all the resources and their relationships. Then I can use this template to deploy this entire resource group together, instead of creating each resource individually. I can also get the code required to deploy this template via different programming languages, or through the Azure scripting tools.

This gives you an idea of why you're seeing two types of virtual machines and other services in the full services list, and why we are always associating resources to resource groups. See Figure 3-33.

Figure 3-33. *Select Resource groups and drill in your resource group to see all of the components associated with it*

So, we've created a virtual machine and connected to it through the portal. Now, we will create and deploy a web application, but instead of doing it from the portal, we will do this from the Visual Studio IDE on your machine.

Web App ASP.NET

Azure App Service Web Apps (or just Web Apps) provides a highly scalable, self-patching web hosting service for hosting web applications, REST APIs, and mobile back ends. You can develop in your favorite language, be it .NET, Node.js, .NET Core, Ruby, Java, Python, or PHP. Applications run and scale with ease. Azure has SDKs in many languages and extensions to popular IDEs, such as Visual Studio and Eclipse. Why Web Apps? We can use a web app to provide access to an SQL database in the cloud, for example. We will create a web application and deploy it to Azure from Visual Studio.

1. Bring up Visual Studio 2017 on your machine (not in the VM we just created).

2. Create an ASP.NET MVC app. Go to File ➤ New Project ➤ Visual C# ➤ Web ➤ ASP.NET Web Application. See Figure 3-34.

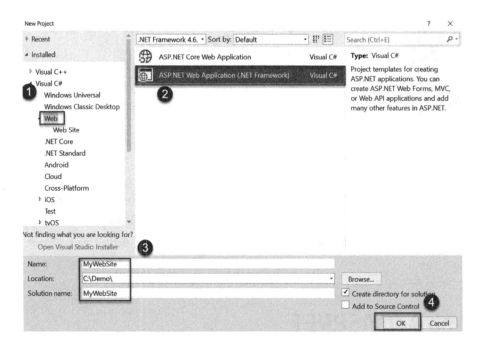

Figure 3-34. *Creating a new Web project in Visual Studio on your machine*

3. Select MVC and click OK. See Figure 3-35.

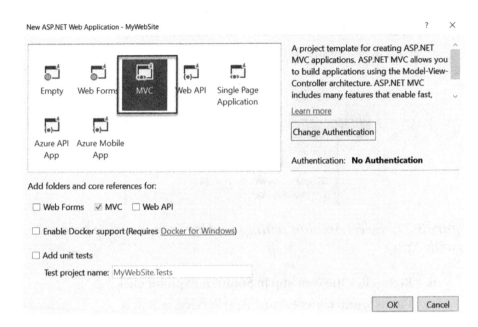

Figure 3-35. *Select MVC*

4. Left-click project and select Build. See Figure 3-36.

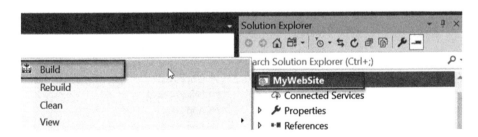

Figure 3-36. *Build the project*

121

5. In the upper-right corner of the Visual Studio IDE, you may have to sign in to your Azure account, in order to publish to the Azure account associated with it. See Figure 3-37.

Figure 3-37. *Select Account settings and log in to the same account as with Azure*

6. Right-click the web app in Solution Explorer click Publish, and choose Azure App Service, which is the service that hosts web applications, mobile back ends, and web APIs in Azure. See Figure 3-38.

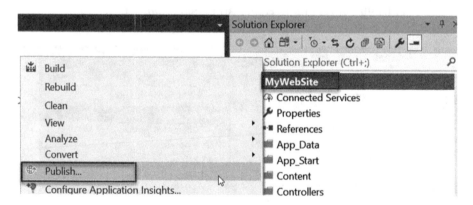

Figure 3-38. *Select Publish*

7. Here, we can choose one of our existing apps or
    create a new one. We will create a new web app, give
    it a name, and create a resource group (which is the
    container of multiple apps used by my application.
    Everything we create for this app will be associated
    with this new group). Finally, click Create. See
    Figures 3-39 and 3-40.

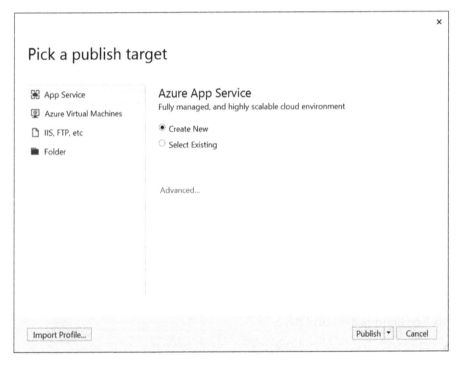

Figure 3-39. *Select Azure App Service, Create New, and Publish*

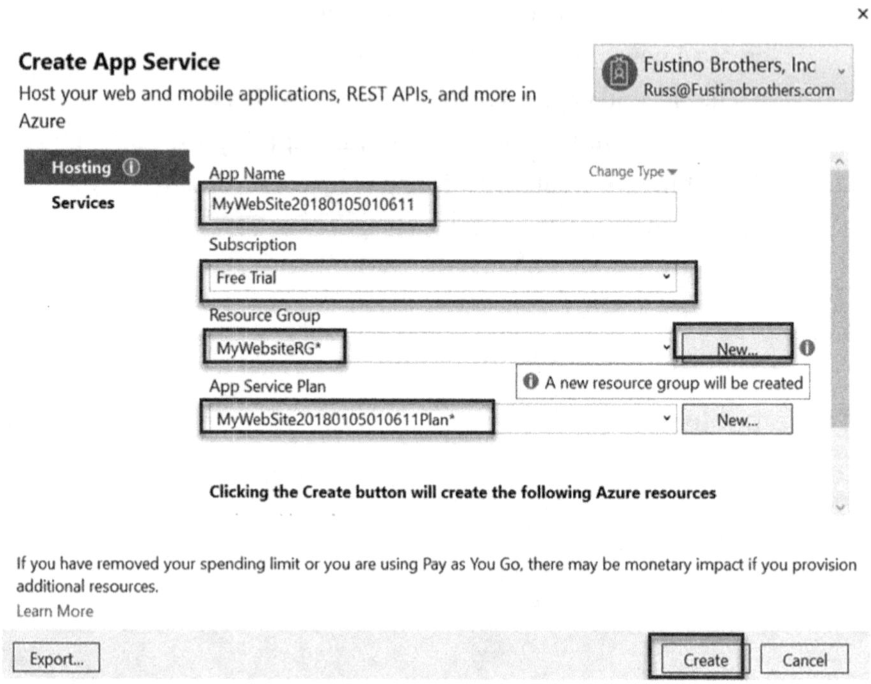

Figure 3-40. *Provide App Name, select Subscription, create new Resource Group (MyWebsiteRG), and keep the App Service Plan default*

Visual Studio is now working with the Azure resource management APIs to create a new web app and will then automatically deploy our web app. See Figures 3-41 and 3-42.

Publish

🖥 **Azure successfully configured:** How was your experience?

| 🔳 MyWebSite20180105010611 - Web Deploy ⌄ | Publish | ⟳ |

Create new profile

Summary

Site URL	http://mywebsite20180105010611.azurewebsites.net ⟎	Settings...
Resource Group	MyWebsiteRG	Preview...
Configuration	Release	Rename profile...
Username	$MyWebSite20180105010611	Delete profile
Password	**********	

Figure 3-41. *Azure is successfully configured*

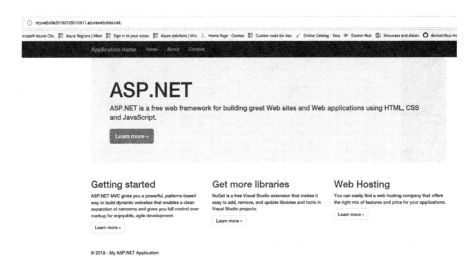

Figure 3-42. *Azure web site is running*

Let's switch over to the Azure portal and see what was created. In the portal, click App services. Another thing we can see here is that the web site is associated with an App Service plan, which is basically the pricing tier, or the features we are paying for. We can see that we are now using

125

the Standard tier, but if we scroll down and click Scale up, we can see the full range of pricing tiers. For example, if we don't require strong compute power but need to associate a custom domain to our web site, we would choose the Standard S1 tier. We could also go with higher tiers, and then our resources are dedicated to us and can be shared among several web sites. We can add backup, SSL, and can load balance across regions and more. For now, let's stay with the free tier. See Figures 3-43 and 3-44.

Figure 3-43. *See associated service plan and click Scale up to see options*

Figure 3-44. *Service plan tiers*

Visual Studio has added a deployment profile file to my project, with information about the app service I am deploying my web app to, so the next time, I'd like to push those changes to Azure. All I must do is hit Publish again. Visual Studio has all the information it requires to deploy it. Click Connected Services under Solution Explorer and click the Publish tab, as shown in Figure 3-45.

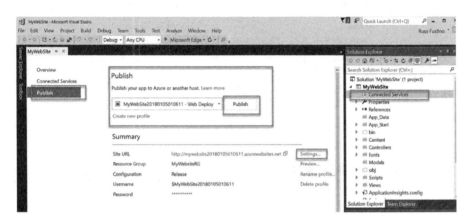

Figure 3-45. *Connected Services are retained*

So, we saw how to create a virtual machine through the portal, and how to create and deploy a web site using Visual Studio. Now, I'd like to show you how you can script it.

Azure CLI

The Azure command-line interface (CLI) has two scripting options. If you're a Windows user and are familiar with PowerShell, Azure has PowerShell cmdlets that let you leverage the rich capabilities that PowerShell provides. If you feel more comfortable in the command line, or are using a Mac or Linux, you can use the cross platform command-line tools to do the same things. Behind the scenes, both Azure PowerShell and the Azure command-line interface interact with the same set of APIs, so the capabilities are very similar. It is a matter of personal choice.

Before I discuss the CLI tools, I am going to show you how to install them on your own machine.

1. Go to `azure.microsoft.com` and, at the bottom of the page, click Downloads. Scroll down to see the CLI tools. See Figures 3-46 and 3-47.

Figure 3-46. *Select Downloads at the bottom of the `azure. microsoft.com` page*

Command-line tools

Manage your Azure services and apps using scripts from the command line.

PowerShell	Azure command-line interface
Windows install	Install
Documentation	Documentation
Browse script center	

Azure Storage Emulator

Install

Documentation

Figure 3-47. *Select PowerShell and command-line installs*

2. Open PowerShell and note a few things we can do
    with the Azure PowerShell tools, as follows:

PowerShell

```
Login-AzureRmAccount
Get-AzureRmSubscription
Select-AzureRMSubscription -SubscriptionName "subname"
New-AzureRmResourceGroup -Name rgfromps -Location "West US"
New-AzureRmAppServicePlan -Name appplanfromps -Location
"West US" -ResourceGroupName rgfromps
New-AzureRmWebApp -Name awesomewebappfromps -Location
"East US" -ResourceGroupName rgfromps -AppServicePlan
appplanfromps
```

3. Within a few seconds, we were able to create a new
    web app running on Azure. See Figures 3-48 and 3-49.

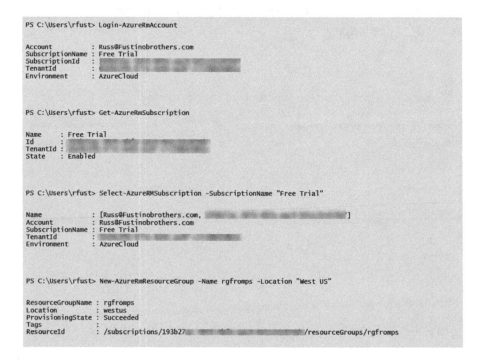

Figure 3-48. *PowerShell commands*

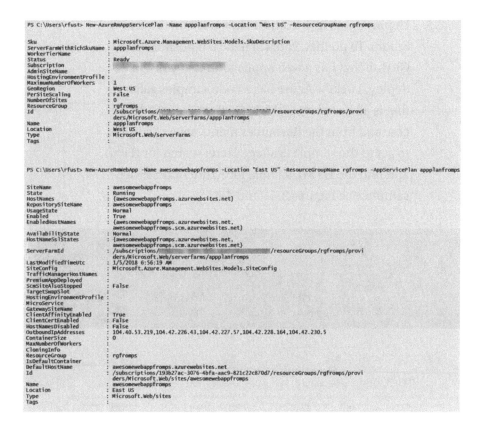

Figure 3-49. *PowerShell commands*

4. Now switch back to the portal and search for that web
    app. In Figure 3-50, you can see that it is associated
    with the plan and resource group we just created.

Figure 3-50. *Web app and service plan created with PowerShell*

5. Deploy a web app from GitHub, not from Visual
    Studio. To do that, you will need a repository on
    GitHub that has a web application that you can
    deploy. Luckily, Azure has a code samples gallery
    that is all based on GitHub. Go to `azure.microsoft.`
    `com`, and from the Resources menu, select Samples,
    to get to the samples gallery. Here, search for HTML
    and find the HTML sample for Azure App Service
    sample. See Figures 3-51 and 3-52.

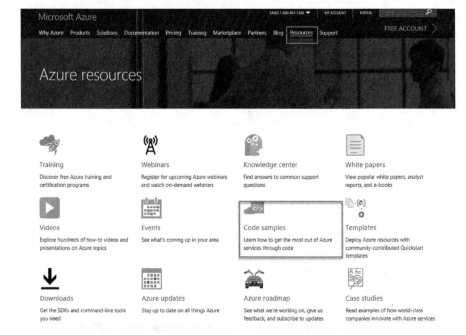

Figure 3-51. *Go to the Resources menu and select Code samples*

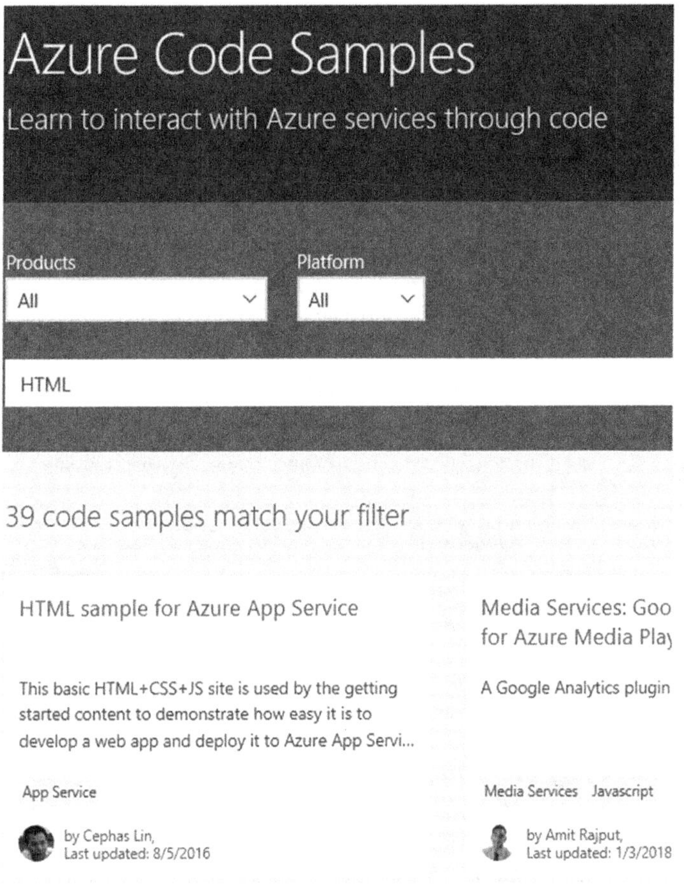

Figure 3-52. Select HTML sample for Azure App Service

6. Browse GitHub and grab the clone URL, as shown in
    Figure 3-53.

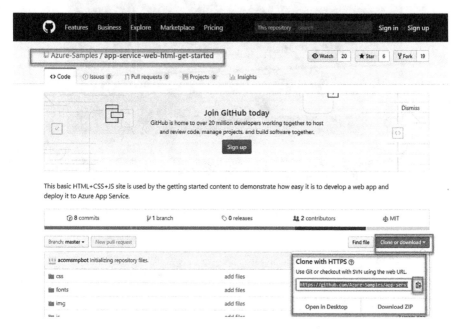

Figure 3-53. *Copy the clone URL*

7. Now, go back to the portal and, on the MVC demo
    web app, select Deployment options, then External
    Repository, and paste that URL. When you click
    Deployment options again, you will see that the
    portal has already deployed that app to your web
    site. See Figures 3-54, 3-55, and 3-56.

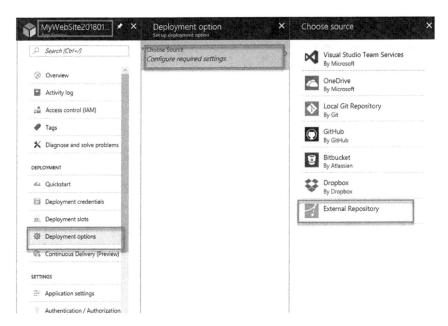

Figure 3-54. *Deployment options for the MVC web site. Select External Repository and paste in the clone URL*

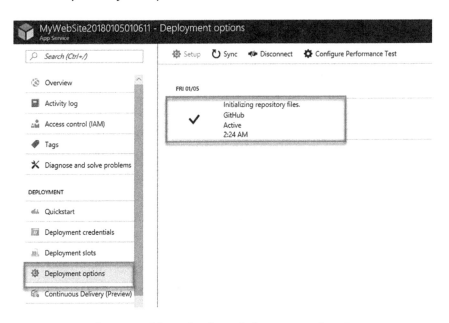

Figure 3-55. *The portal has deployed the app to the site*

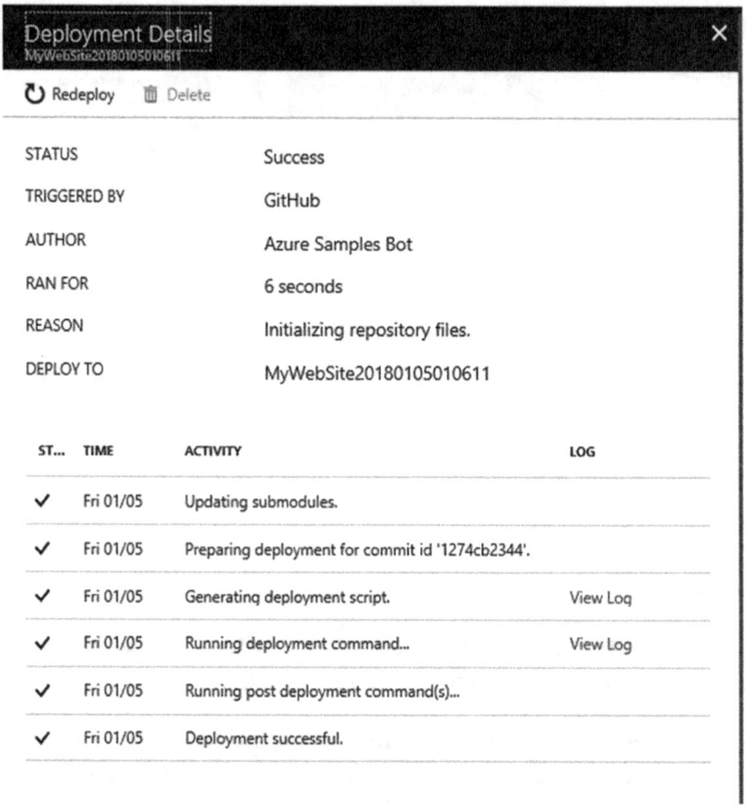

Figure 3-56. *Deployment details*

There are a few more things you can do with
your web apps through the portal. You can set up
backups, scale them up, scale them out, configure
a custom domain name, set up SSL, set SSL up for
security scanning, and even visit a live console and
explore your application in production—all within
that rich Azure portal.

On the web site blade, and, if you are a DevOps person and
want to keep an eye on the site's metrics, you can consult the
chart in Figure 3-57.

8. Click and add more metrics that you are interested
    in, such as the number of 200 requests, 404s, and
    more. You can even take this chart and pin it to your
    main dashboard and make it your personal DevOps
    dashboard, with all the information you require on
    your running services. In fact, you can click Edit
    dashboard and customize this dashboard the way
    you want.

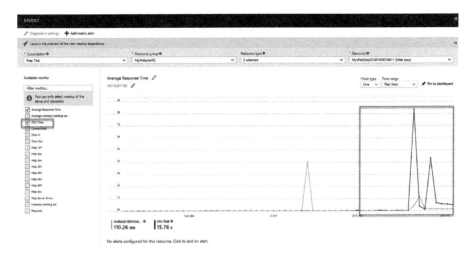

Figure 3-57. *Click any chart and add metrics, by clicking items on
the left. Here CPU Time has been added.*

So, we've created a VM and some web apps. Now we need a database.

SQL Database

There are two ways you can run SQL databases on Azure. You can install
SQL Server on a VM and get full control over the configuration of the
database. In fact, SQL Server running on a VM is one of the most popular
things people do on Azure.

Another way is to use the Azure SQL Database service, which lets you create your database in seconds, without having to take care of any infrastructure or manage software updates.

Creating Your Database

To create an SQL database in Azure, we can take the same approaches we've seen before. We can create it from the portal or enlist the Azure CLI or PowerShell to do it. We will use the portal.

1. Click New, and from the database category, choose SQL Database. See Figure 3-58.

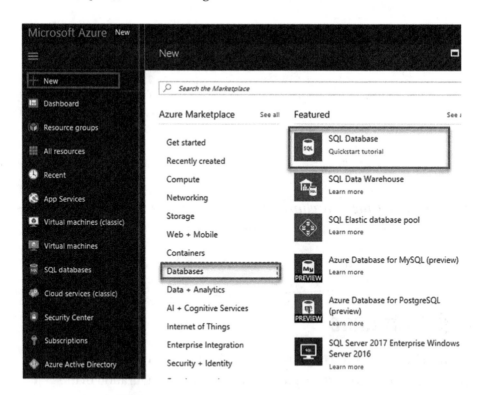

Figure 3-58. *Click +New ➤ Databases and select SQL Database*

2. Give it a name (SQL2018) and create a new resource group. We can create our database as a new empty database, seed it with sample data, or create it from a backup that may have been created earlier. Here we are selecting the source as a Sample AdventureWorks database. This could also be the easiest way to move your databases to the cloud. Just upload a backup and create a database from it. We can create a new database server (that can hold multiple database instances) and choose a location with credentials. See Figure 3-59. For the credentials, use the following:

    `demoadmin, Demo@pass123`

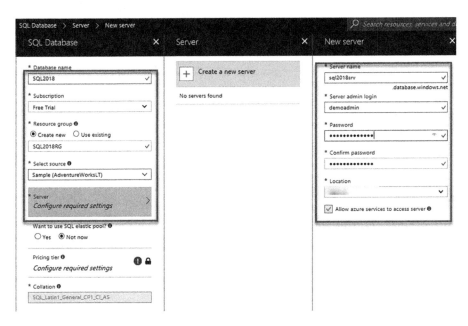

Figure 3-59. *Enter database name, select subscription, select sample date, create a new resource group called SQL2018RG, configure server with name sql2018srv, and provide credentials*

3. Choose a pricing tier. As you can see, you can play around with SQL databases for as little as $5 per month, at the lowest performance tier. SQL databases use DTUs—data transaction units—as a performance measurement. So, as you check out the different pricing tiers, this is the number you should pay the most attention to. As your solution grows, you can scale your database and change your pricing tier at any point, without any downtime. See Figure 3-60.

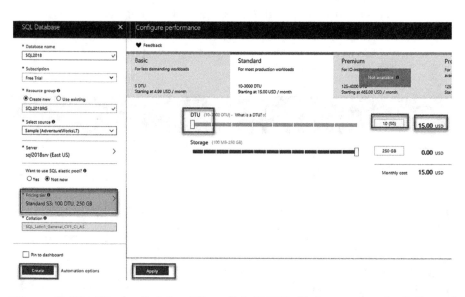

Figure 3-60. *Under Pricing Tier, slide DTU all the way to the left, and you will see the current cost. Here it is $15.00 per month for 250GB of storage. Click Create and Apply.*

4. Provisioning a database can take a few minutes, and you can check the notification area in the portal to get the latest update. Once the database is provisioned, you can start monitoring it. You can set up geo-replication, scale it up to a different tier, based on your performance needs, configure security, and more.

5. Open SQL2018 after it deploys. To access it on the server we just created for the database, add white list IP addresses by clicking Set server firewall rules. Add client IP and save. This will allow access to your IP or IP addresses range. Click save. Now you can connect through a client library or SDK or a management tool. Azure SQL Database allows you to connect to it from a variety of programing languages, such as .NET, Java, PHP, Python, and more. See Figures 3-61 and 3-62.

Figure 3-61. *Select Set server firewall*

Figure 3-62. *Click Add client IP, then Save*

Let's connect to this database, to see the sample data that was populated into the database, and run queries against it.

Using Visual Studio to Verify Your Database

After you have created a database, the next thing you will want to do is see the sample data that you seeded it with. In the following steps, we will bring up Server Explorer and connect to the Azure database and then view the data using the SQL Server Object Explorer.

1. Open Visual Studio, navigate to Server Explorer, and connect to Microsoft Azure Subscription. See Figure 3-63.

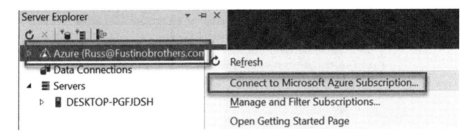

Figure 3-63. *From Server Explorer, right-click Azure and select Connect to Microsoft Azure Subscription*

2. Expand the database and right-click and select Open in SQL Server Object Explorer. See Figure 3-64.

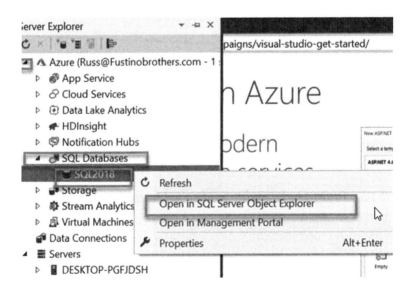

Figure 3-64. *From Server Explorer, expand SQL Databases, Right click on SQL2018 and select Open in SQL Server Object Explorer*

3. Query the existing table by right-clicking the
    database table and selecting View Data. See
    Figures 3-65 and 3-66.

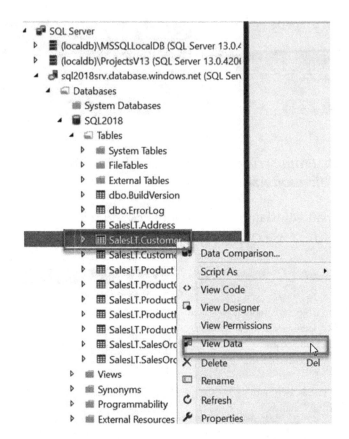

Figure 3-65. *Right-click a table and select View Data*

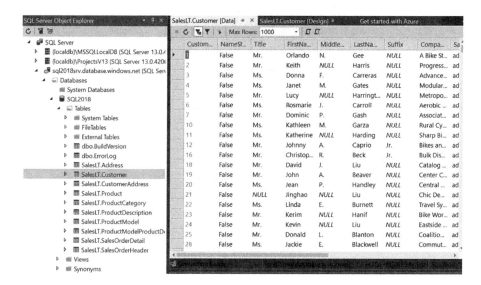

Figure 3-66. *Rows for the table are retrieved and displayed*

Building Solutions

Awesome! So, we've created a virtual machine, deployed web apps, and created an SQL database in Azure. This should allow us to start building solutions today, using your free trial accounts.

Documentation

To learn more about the different Azure services, there is a huge documentation section available from `azure.microsoft.com`.

1. If you click on the Documentation link at the top menu bar, you can browse through all the services and dive into their documentation. You can also get high-level white papers for developers and IT operators that provide a good technical overview of the platform and services and when to choose which service, based on the scenario you're building. See Figure 3-67.

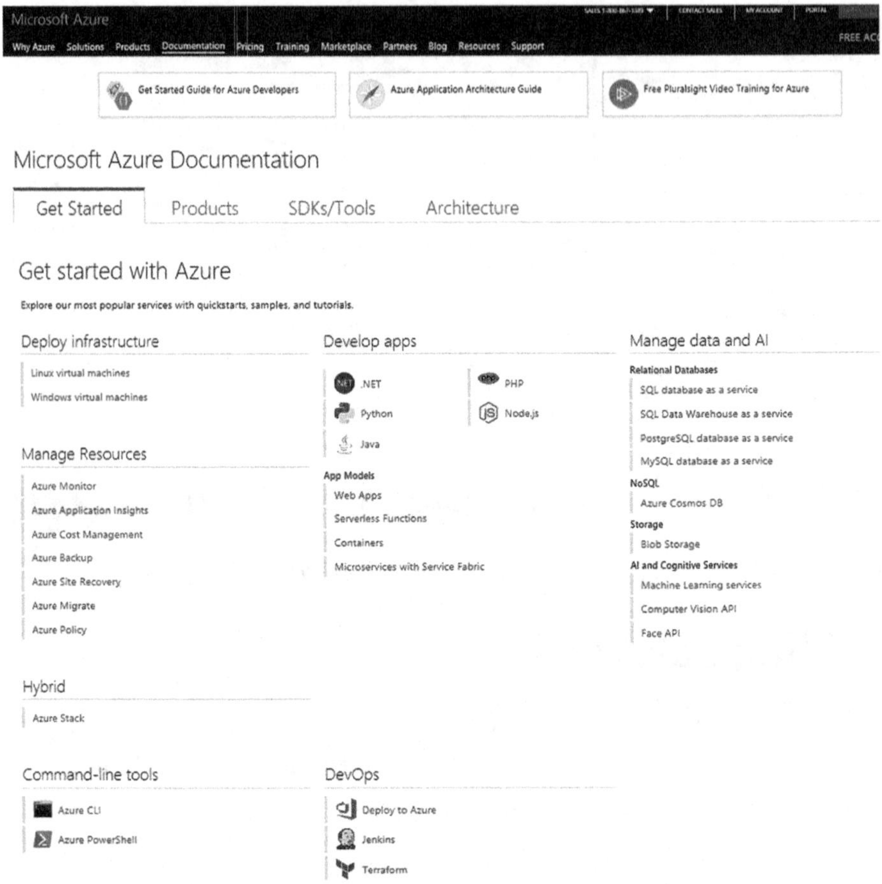

Figure 3-67.   *Select documentation from Microsoft Azure*

Solutions

In many cases, your solutions are going to be composed of multiple services. For example, if you're building a digital marketing web site, you might start with a web site and scale it to different parts of the world, using Traffic Manager, move your content to a CDN, and service media with Media Services. If you visit the Solutions area on Microsoft Azure, you'll find the information you need to do that.

1. Navigate to `https://azure.microsoft.com/en-us/ solutions/`. Here are some of the types of solutions customers are building on Azure today. Click Digital Marketing, for example, and you can see some key benefits, learn about the core Azure services that can help you, and, if you scroll down to the bottom, you'll see some architectures for common scenarios. See Figures 3-68 and 3-69.

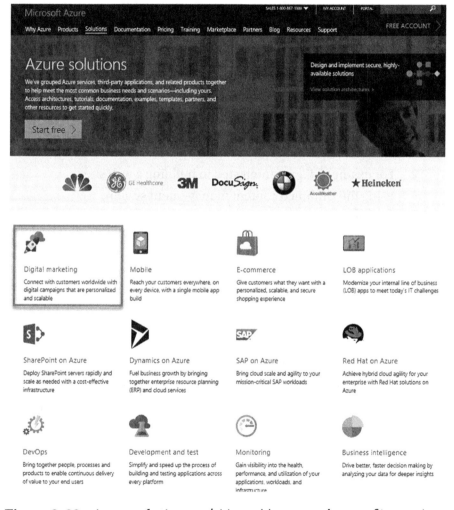

Figure 3-68. *Azure solutions at* `https://azure.microsoft.com/ en-us/solutions/`

Solution architecture: Scalable Episerver marketing website

Let your business run multi-channel digital marketing websites on one platform and spin up and spin down campaigns on demand. Take advantage of the comprehensive capabilities of Episerver to manage every aspect of your site and campaign performance.

This solution is built on the Azure managed services: Traffic Manager, Content Delivery Network, SQL Database, Redis Cache and Application Insights. These services run in a high-availability environment, patched and supported, allowing you to focus on your solution instead of the environment they run in.

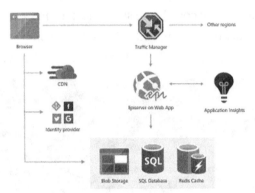

Figure 3-69. *One of the solution diagrams for digital marketing*

2. For example, if I am interested in building a web site using the Umbraco content management system, I can get an architecture diagram that shows me all the services I need to use and how they should be composed together. I can also see related documentation to help me get started.

Status

If you're starting to think about production services on Azure, another useful page is the Status page, easily found on the footer under Support, that shows you the health of the platform and if there's any known issues for services or regions.

1. Navigate to https://azure.microsoft.com/en-us/
    status/. We all know that every software has bugs,
    and hardware might fail, so if you're seeing something
    weird, I suggest going to this page and detecting if
    there is anything going on. See Figure 3-70.

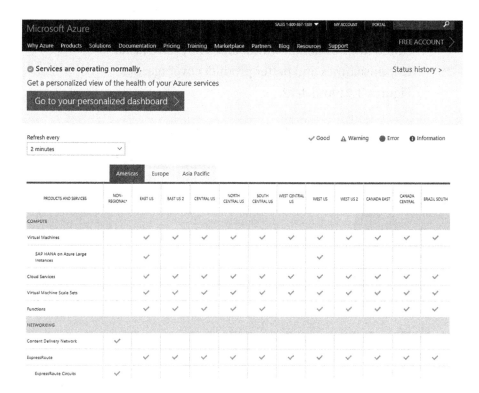

Figure 3-70. *Check status at* https://azure.microsoft.com/
en-us/status/.

Support

What about support? As you're going through the phases of testing out the technology all the way to running production workloads in the cloud, you might want to consider getting some level of support. It is nice to know that there are options, depending on your needs and budget. Let's compare some.

1. On Microsoft Azure, click Support and then
   Compare Support Plans. The free support you're
   getting as part of the free trial account covers billing
   and subscription-related issues. The developer
   support plan is great if you're playing around with
   the technology and require technical assistance. The
   standard and professional support plans are best
   suited for production workloads. They have faster
   response times and better product coverage. See
   Figures 3-71 and 3-72.

Figure 3-71. *On Microsoft Azure, click Support and then Compare Support Plans*

Plan comparison

AZURE SUPPORT PLANS	INCLUDED WITH AZURE	DEVELOPER	STANDARD	PROFESSIONAL DIRECT	PREMIER
		Upgrade support	Upgrade support	Upgrade support	Contact Premier
Best for:	Billing and subscription support; online self-help	Trial and non-production environments	Production workload environments	Business-critical dependence	Substantial dependence across multiple products
Range of support	Microsoft Azure	Microsoft Azure	Microsoft Azure	Microsoft Azure	All Microsoft products
Twitter @AzureSupport & Forums¹	✓	✓	✓	✓	✓
Technical support for Azure service issues via Resource health²,³	✓	✓	✓	✓	✓
Azure Stack support included			✓	✓	✓
Unlimited 24x7 billing & subscription support	✓	✓	✓	✓	✓

Figure 3-72. *View your support options*

2. To open a support request, you simply go to the Azure portal and start the process. See Figures 3-73 and 3-74.

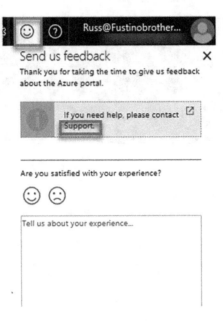

Figure 3-73. *Click the smiley face and then Support*

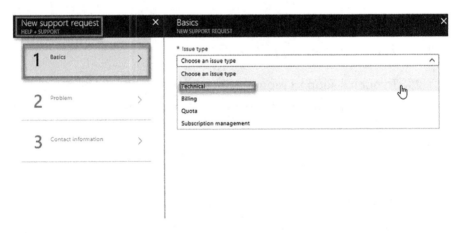

Figure 3-74. *Fill out a new support request*

Delete Resources

When learning Azure, it is a good idea to delete resources you created in the learning process. By doing so, you will extend the Azure credits. You have used a couple of dollars' worth in this chapter, if you completed it in a few hours. These resources will not be required for the remainder of the book.

1. Delete the resources created in this chapter, by clicking Resource groups, then pressing the delete button for each of them. The resources should be related to demorg, MyWebsiteRG, rgfromps, and, the latest, SQL2018RG. See Figures 3-75 and 3-76.

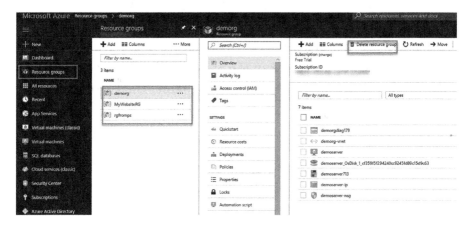

Figure 3-75. *Delete resources related to demorg, MyWebsiteRG, and rgfromps*

Figure 3-76. *Delete resources related to SQL2018RG*

Summary

In this chapter, you took the first steps in working with Azure. I discussed free trial accounts and what you can do with them to explore the platform. We used the Azure portal to create and manage resources. We created virtual machines, web apps, and an SQL database and discussed basic concepts, such as resource groups, DTUs, and more. Then we deployed a web app from Visual Studio and saw the tools and the integration we have for Azure inside the IDE. We used scripting tools, such as the Azure CLI and Azure PowerShell, to automate tasks, such as creating a new web app, so we could deploy into it from GitHub. I also discussed growing your solutions and how to find useful resources on azure.microsoft.com related to support, architectures, and more and how to delete learning resources.

CHAPTER 4

Building an Azure Service Using Quickstart

In building a typical app, you need data. Then, you usually have to serve that data up in a web service, so it can be consumed by any client application. Finally, in the client app itself, you must download that data, possibly update it, and send it back. What I have just described are the basic steps in the Quickstart Azure Mobile App.

This chapter is divided into six parts, each of which represents a main task in creating an Azure service, beginning with Quickstart. You will use the Azure portal to create a mobile app, using Xamarin Forms Quickstart, and Quickstart will create a database for the app. Quickstart also allows you to create an app service, using the Table API. Finally, Quickstart generates a sample Xamarin Forms application to consume the data. Quickstart creates one table, which represents a "to do item" list. The Xamarin Forms app created will display and update the "to do item" table.

This is great! However, realistically, the next thing you will have to do is add your own tables to your own application. I will cover how to do this in this chapter as well. You will then modify the Table API service app and, in Chapter 5, create two additional tables for a different app to consume. This first table is for questions, with a list of possible answers for each question,

© Russell Fustino 2018

R. Fustino, *Azure and Xamarin Forms*, https://doi.org/10.1007/978-1-4842-3561-4_4

and is called Questions. This is analogous to a multiple-choice question on an exam. The user will respond to those questions by selecting an answer, and that response will be stored in the second table, called Responses. The data that gets generated for the Questions table will be accomplished in this chapter. The data that gets generated for the Responses table will be generated in Chapter 5. In other words, this chapter will focus primarily on the app service, and the next chapter will focus primarily on the client.

The result will be to consume the Questions table in a client app that serves as a polling service to the user community. The Xamarin client app will display the question and ask the user to select a desired answer from a list and then store the response. It is kind of like a voting system in which each user of the app will be responding to a question. For example, to a question such as "What is your favorite book in the list?", the user would select from the list the book he or she likes best. This will be referred to as a polling app. As part of this process, you will have to seed the data for the questions and a list of possible answers to select from. Finally, we will verify that seeded data generated in this chapter is stored in the "to do item" table from Quickstart as well as the customized Questions table.

Note   Run the code in this chapter from your laptop/PC and *not* an Azure virtual machine.

Time Estimate
60 Minutes

Part 1: Create a Mobile App in the Azure Portal

Time Estimate

10 Minutes

Let's get started. In this part, we will begin the process of creating a mobile app in the Azure portal. We must do this first, because Quickstart becomes available on one of the blades, once the mobile app is deployed. We will then cover the first step in Quickstart for mobile app Xamarin Forms, which is used to create the database. We will then perform a second step in Quickstart, which is to download the code required for the API service.

1. From `http://portal.azure.com`, click New, then Web + Mobile. Next, select Mobile App. See Figure 4-1.

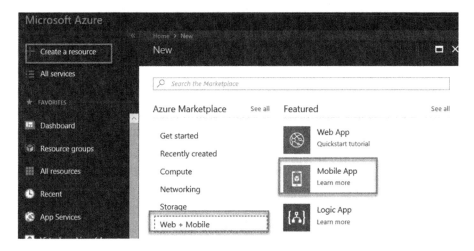

Figure 4-1. *From the Azure portal, click New, Web + Mobile, and select Mobile App*

2. Create a new mobile app with a unique app name
   like BookPollApp and a new resource group called
   BookPollAppRG. Select or create an app service plan
   in a location close to you. (use this same location for
   all future resources). Click OK and then Create new,
   as shown in Figure 4-2. It will take about a minute to
   create the new mobile app.

Figure 4-2. *Create a new mobile app with a unique app
name similar to BookPollApp and a new resource group called
BookPollAppRG*

3. Once notified, the app is created, and if it does not
   open automatically, open the service manually.
   On the App Service blade, select Quickstart and
   Xamarin.Forms, as shown in Figure 4-3.

Figure 4-3. *Select Quickstart and Xamarin.Forms*

4. You will see that there are three steps:

    a. Connect a Database

    b. Create a Table API

    c. Configure Your Client Application (Xamarin Forms)

    Execute one step at a time and wait for the deployments for each step to finish before proceeding to the next step. The app we are writing will be a polling service with questions provided in the app service (step 2) and selected answers provided in the app client (covered in Chapter 5). We will look at the Quickstart app generated for the client application, which displays a "to do list" in Step 3.

5.   Click the information box to connect a database, as
     the first step in the Quickstart wizard. See Figure 4-4.

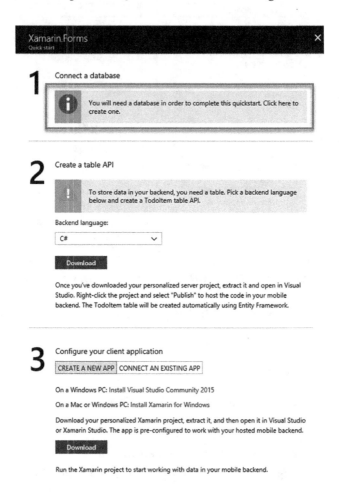

Figure 4-4. *Select Connect a database*

6.   Click +Add to add a connection. See Figure 4-5.

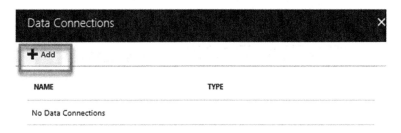

Figure 4-5. *Add a data connection*

7.   Click SQL Database *Configure required settings* ➤
+ Create a new database, give it a unique name like
BookPollAppDB, and click Target server *Configure
required settings.* Give the server a unique name,
such as bookpollappsrv, and type "demouser" as
the server admin login, "Demo@pass123" (case
sensitive) as the password, and then the desired
location, as in Figure 4-6. Accept the default pricing
tier of Standard s0: 10 DTU, 250GB, then click Select.

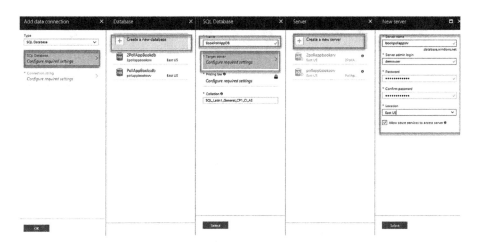

Figure 4-6. *Create a new database and new server with the
properties illustrated here*

8. Click *MS_TableConnectionString*, as in Figure 4-7, and accept the default name. Click OK to start the database deployment.

Figure 4-7. *Accept the default connection string name*

9. The deployment will take three or four minutes. Once created, proceed to step 2 of Quickstart from the portal, but only after the data connection is created. (It is important that you wait, or it may not work.) Once you see the green check mark in step 1, proceed to step 2. Time for a coffee. See Figure 4-8.

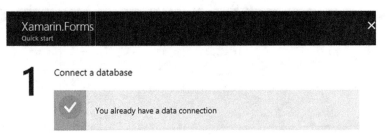

Figure 4-8. *Wait until you see the green check mark in step 1 before proceeding to step 2*

10. Now that you have successfully created a database, click C# from the drop-down menu and then click Download. Download to a folder close to your root drive, such as C:\apressbook. See Figure 4-9.

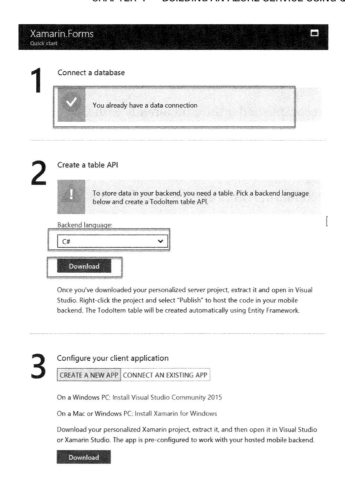

Figure 4-9. *Select C# from the drop-down menu and then click Download*

Do not close the portal window with Quickstart showing. We will return to it in about 20 minutes, to complete step 3. If you try to perform step 3 now, it will fail for the rest of this chapter. Be patient; trust me here.

Part 2: Modify the Service App

Time Estimate

5 Minutes

We have accomplished quite a bit already with steps 1 and 2 of Quickstart completed. We created a database and generated the code required to serve it up in an API service. In theory, all we have to do is compile and publish the app service and then perform step 3 to download the Xamarin Forms app. HOWEVER, WE ARE NOT GOING TO DO THIS YET. The reason? I want to show you how to work with your own Xamarin Forms application, not just the app generated from Quickstart. In other words, Quickstart is great for creating a new application (we are going to do that in due time in this chapter), but we are going to kill two birds with one stone and also cover how to modify the API service to provide data for an existing app, by generating a couple of new tables before we publish this service. Those two additional tables will be used in the app in Chapter 5. In this part, you will modify the Table API Service app generated with Quickstart, to add those two new tables.

Caution   Do not publish this until all the modifications have been made and you are directed to do so toward the end of this chapter.

Note   The completed solution is provided at `https://github.com/Apress/azure-and-xamarin-forms` however the Chapter 4 solution is for reference only. The Quickstart created solution places the correct end point in the code as well as the configuration settings. So, the provided solution will not run and publish successfully, as is.

---

1. Once downloaded, in File Explorer, right-click the zip, select properties, check unblock, and click OK. Extract the files. See Figure 4-10.

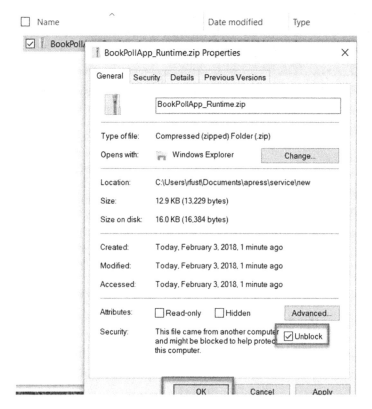

Figure 4-10. *Check Unblock and click OK*

2. Open the solution in Visual Studio, right-click the solution, select Restore NuGet Packages, and then rebuild the solution. See Figure 4-11.

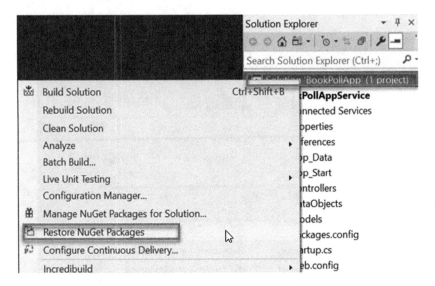

Figure 4-11. *Right-click the solution and select Restore NuGet Packages*

3. Open the BookPollAppService solution.

4. Right-click the solution and select Manage NuGet Packages, then browse to add the package for System.ComponentModel.Annotations. See Figure 4-12.

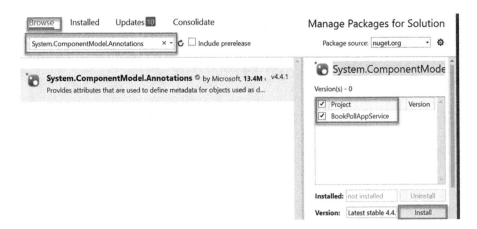

Figure 4-12. *Browse for System.ComponentModel.Annotations and install*

The plumbing is done, with the code and NuGet packages installed. Now, let's get down to adding two new tables to the Service API in the next part.

Part 3: Add the Question and Response DTOs and End Points

Time Estimate

5 Minutes

In this part, we will prepare the app to seed the Questions table with data the first time we access it. This will require that you create a class to represent this, both in our database and over the wire, when talking to a client. You will add a class named PollQuestion to provide this support. You will also need to add a new TableController, to expose this table over the network. You want to store this object in a table named "questions". The JSON format will match the data transformation object (DTO). The JSON parser will automatically lowercase the property names.

1. Add a class to the DataObjects folder called PollQuestion. See Figure 4-13.

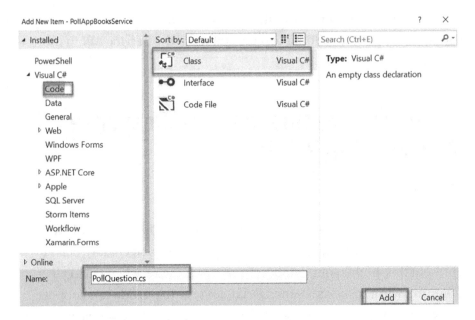

Figure 4-13. *Add a class and name it* `PollQuestion.cs` *in the* `DataObjects` *folder*

2. Add the following using statements:

```
using Microsoft.Azure.Mobile.Server;
using System.ComponentModel.DataAnnotations.Schema;
```

3. Derive the class from `EntityData` and add code for Text and Answers. The highlighted text represents code changes.

```
namespace BookPollAppService.DataObjects
{
    [Table("questions")]
    public class PollQuestion : EntityData
    {
        public string Text { get; set; }
```

```
        public string Answers { get; set; }
    }

}
```

4. Add a class to the DataObjects folder called PollResponse.

5. Add the using statements:

```
using System.ComponentModel.DataAnnotations.Schema;
using Microsoft.Azure.Mobile.Server;
using Newtonsoft.Json;
```

6. Add a class to the DataObjects folder called PollResponse. Add the following code:

```
namespace BookPollAppService.DataObjects
{
    [Table("responses")]
    public class PollResponse : EntityData
    {
        [JsonProperty("questionId")]
        public string QuestionId { get; set; }

        public string Name { get; set; }
        [JsonProperty("answer")]
        public int AnswerIndex { get; set; }
    }

}
```

7. Save all.

We have now completed the DTOs thatdefine our new tables. Let's now expose the data, through functions on retrieving and updating the tables, by creating the controllers.

Part 4: Add Controllers

Time Estimate

20 Minutes

In this part, you will wire up controllers to expose a table over the wire. The question table controller should expose only the GET options (all or by ID). We will not allow this table to be updated in the client Xamarin Forms app.

Using a database initializer function, we will seed this table with data, by creating a set of poll questions and inserting them into it.

1. **Try** { Right-click the `Controllers` folder and select Add ➤ Controller, then select Azure Mobile Apps Table Controller. See Figures 4-14 and 4-15.

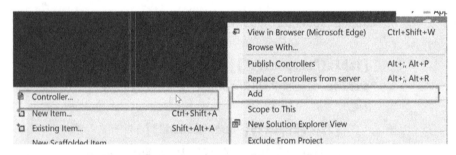

Figure 4-14. *Right-click the* `Controllers` *folder and select Add Controller*

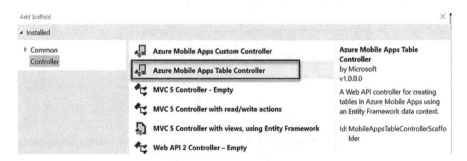

Figure 4-15. *Select Azure Mobile Apps Table Controller*

2. Try: { Select PollQuestion from the Model class
    drop-down menu and BookPollAppService for the
    Data context class. Rename the default controller
    to QuestionsController. You will also have to add
    a controller for PollResponse, using a controller.
    Revise the default name to ResponsesController.

3. Try: { Select PollQuestion from the Model class
    drop-down menu, BookPollAppContext from
    the Data context class drop-down, and rename
    PollQuestionController QuetionsController (See
    possible error in step 5 below). See Figure 4-16.

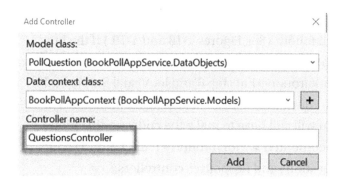

Figure 4-16. *Controller renamed QuestionsController*

4. Try: { PollResponse from the Model class drop-down,
    insert BookPollAppContext as the Data context
    class, and change the name of the Controller from
    PollResponseController to ResonsesController
    (See possible error in step 5 below). See Figure 4-17.

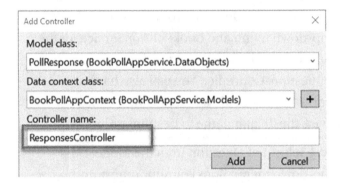

Figure 4-17. *Controller renamed ResponsesController*

5. Catch: { If you get either of the following errors related to scaffolding, resulting from a known bug in VS 2017 at the time of writing, see the workarounds that follow. (See Figures 4-18 and 4-19.) If the bug is fixed by the time you read this, simply follow workaround #1 at step 6 and let Visual Studio add the controllers instead of adding them manually. You will still have to make the code modifications documented in workaround #1, after adding your Questions and Responses controllers.

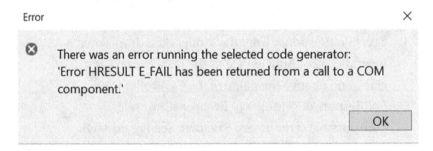

Figure 4-18. *COM component error*

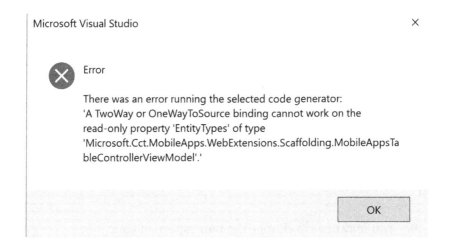

Microsoft Visual Studio   ✕

Error

There was an error running the selected code generator:
'A TwoWay or OneWayToSource binding cannot work on the
read-only property 'EntityTypes' of type
'Microsoft.Cct.MobileApps.WebExtensions.Scaffolding.MobileAppsTa
bleControllerViewModel'.'

OK

Figure 4-19. *Scaffolding error*

}

6. **Catch** {There are two workarounds.}

7. Workaround #1 is quicker, unless you already have
   VS 2015 installed, as VS 2015 can take a couple
   of hours to install. Workaround #1 is to add the
   classes and code modifications manually in step
   6. Workaround #2 starts at step 13 and is about
   reverting to VS 2015 and installing the Azure SDK for
   VS 2015, to create the table controllers. Once added
   successfully, return to using VS 2017. If you use
   workaround #2, you will still have to make the code
   modifications in steps 7 through 12. Details on each
   workaround follow.

8. Workaround #1

   Add an existing file from the book assets folder
   called `QuestionsController.cs` to the `Controllers`
   folder in the project solution, only if you received
   one of the preceding errors. See Figure 4-20.

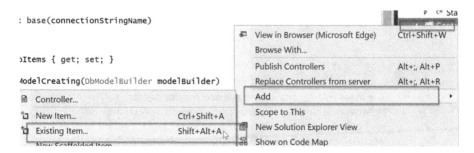

Figure 4-20. *Add* QuestionsController.cs *to the* Controllers *folder*

9. You may have to change the namespace of your project name, and you should remove or comment any "non-GET" methods, as the question data will be read-only. So, comment out or delete the tasks for PATCH, POST, and DELETE questions.

10. The code final code should look like the following (resolve the using statements):

```
using System.Linq;
using System.Threading.Tasks;
using System.Web.Http;
using System.Web.Http.Controllers;
using System.Web.Http.OData;
using Microsoft.Azure.Mobile.Server;
using BookPollAppService.DataObjects;
using BookPollAppService.Models;

namespace BookPollAppService.Controllers
{
    public class QuestionsController :
    TableController<PollQuestion>
    {
```

```
protected override void Initialize(HttpController
Context controllerContext)
{
    base.Initialize(controllerContext);
    BookPollAppContext context = new
    BookPollAppContext();
    DomainManager = new EntityDomainManager<
    PollQuestion>(context, Request);
}

// GET tables/PollQuestion
public IQueryable<PollQuestion>
GetAllPollQuestion()
{
    return Query();
}

// GET tables/PollQuestion/48D68C86-6EA6-4C25-
AA33-223FC9A27959
public SingleResult<PollQuestion>
GetPollQuestion(string id)
{
    return Lookup(id);
}
}
}
```

11. Add an existing file for the student materials to the
    Controllers folder, called ResponsesController.cs.
    You may have to change the namespace to your
    project name.

12. We can customize it with ASP.NET attributes. For example, we can rename the methods to match what they do.

- Rename the PostPollResponse method to InsertPollResponse. Because we no longer have the word "Post" on the method, the controller will not associate this to an HTTP POST request. To correct this, add an [HttpPost] attribute to the method.

- Rename the PatchPollResponse method to UpdatePollResponse and add an [HttpPatch] attribute to the method, to ensure that it responds to an HTTP PATCH request.

```
using System.Linq;
using System.Threading.Tasks;
using System.Web.Http;
using System.Web.Http.Controllers;
using System.Web.Http.OData;
using Microsoft.Azure.Mobile.Server;
using BookPollAppService.DataObjects;
using BookPollAppService.Models;

namespace BookPollAppService.Controllers
{
    public class ResponsesController :
    TableController<PollResponse>
    {
        protected override void Initialize(Http
        ControllerContext controllerContext)
        {
```

```
    base.Initialize(controllerContext);
    BookPollAppContext context = new
    BookPollAppContext();
    DomainManager = new EntityDomainManager
    <PollResponse>(context, Request);
}

// GET tables/PollResponse
public IQueryable<PollResponse>
GetAllPollResponse()
{
    return Query();
}

// GET tables/PollResponse/48D68C86-6EA6-
4C25-AA33-223FC9A27959
public SingleResult<PollResponse>
GetPollResponse(string id)
{
    return Lookup(id);
}

// PATCH tables/PollResponse/48D68C86-6EA6-
4C25-AA33-223FC9A27959
[HttpPatch]
public Task<PollResponse>
UpdatePollResponse(string id,
Delta<PollResponse> patch)
{
    return UpdateAsync(id, patch);
}
```

```
// POST tables/PollResponse
[HttpPost]
public async Task<IHttpActionResult>
InsertPollResponse(PollResponse item)
{
    PollResponse current = await
    InsertAsync(item);
    return CreatedAtRoute("Tables", new {
    id = current.Id }, current);
}

// DELETE tables/PollResponse/48D68C86-
6EA6-4C25-AA33-223FC9A27959
public Task DeletePollResponse(string id)
{
        return DeleteAsync(id);
}
    }
}
```

13. Open BookPollAppContext.cs in the Models folder,
    if you manually added the preceding controllers,
    and add these two lines after the OnModelCreating
    method. Also, replace the BookPollAppService
    namespace and lines below with the name of your
    project, if different, and do the same for any using
    statements. These lines may be there already, if you
    successfully added a controller through the Visual
    Studio Add Controller.

```
public System.Data.Entity.DbSet<BookPollAppService.
DataObjects.PollQuestion> PollQuestions { get; set; }

public System.Data.Entity.DbSet<BookPollAppService.
DataObjects.PollResponse> PollResponses { get; set; }
```

14. For BookPollAppContext.cs, the code should look like that shown in Figure 4-21. This completes the controller updates!

```csharp
using System.Data.Entity;
using System.Data.Entity.ModelConfiguration.Conventions;
using System.Linq;
using Microsoft.Azure.Mobile.Server;
using Microsoft.Azure.Mobile.Server.Tables;
using BookPollAppService.DataObjects;

namespace BookPollAppService.Models
{
    public class BookPollAppContext : DbContext
    {
        // You can add custom code to this file. Changes will not be overwritten.
        //
        // If you want Entity Framework to alter your database
        // automatically whenever you change your model schema, please use data migrations.
        // For more information refer to the documentation:
        // http://msdn.microsoft.com/en-us/data/jj591621.aspx

        private const string connectionStringName = "Name=MS_TableConnectionString";

        public BookPollAppContext() : base(connectionStringName)
        {
        }

        public DbSet<TodoItem> TodoItems { get; set; }

        protected override void OnModelCreating(DbModelBuilder modelBuilder)
        {
            modelBuilder.Conventions.Add(
                new AttributeToColumnAnnotationConvention<TableColumnAttribute, string>(
                    "ServiceTableColumn", (property, attributes) => attributes.Single().ColumnType.ToString()));
        }

        public System.Data.Entity.DbSet<BookPollAppService.DataObjects.PollQuestion> PollQuestions { get; set; }

        public System.Data.Entity.DbSet<BookPollAppService.DataObjects.PollResponse> PollResponses { get; set; }
    }
}
```

Figure 4-21. *The completed code for BookPollAppContext.cs*

15.   Workaround # 2

Download and install VS 2015 at www.visualstudio.
com/vs/older-downloads/. You can add controllers
in VS 2015 and go back to a prior version on the Azure
SDK for 2.9.6 and Azure Mobile apps SDK version
2.0.40201. You may have to uninstall the Azure Mobile
Apps SDK first, if newer. This is a bug with the version
of the Azure Mobile Apps SDK installers included
with VS 2017. The templates themselves shouldn't
have changed, so the specific workaround is to
download the Azure 2.9.6 SDK from www.microsoft.
com/en-us/download/details.aspx?id=54289 and
select the AzureMobileAppsSdkV2.0.msi installer
(version 2.0.40201). This will install the scaffolded
controllers to the folder indicated in the error
message. Also, you may have to install the Azure
SDK for VS 2015, which can be accessed at https://
azure.microsoft.com/en-us/downloads/, as shown
in Figures 4-22 and 4-23.

Repeat steps 1–11, to create the controllers,
with the only difference being that you will not
have to add the PollQuestionController and
PollResponseController classes in step 6 from
existing files, as these will have been generated.
Modify generated code as in steps 1–11.

Figure 4-22. *Download the Azure SDK for VS 2015*

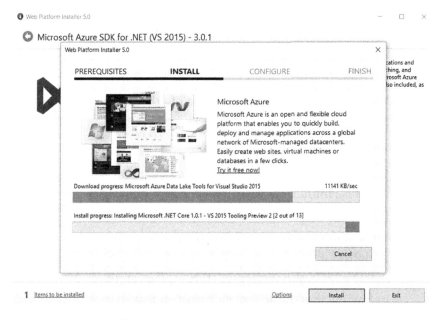

Figure 4-23. *Install the Azure SDK for VS 2015*

We are almost at the finish line! The only thing left in building our API service is to prepopulate our tables with some data. This is referred to as "seeding the data."

Part 5: Seed the Data and Force Entity Framework to Re-create Our Tables and Publish

Time Estimate

10 Minutes

When you ship an application, it is often required that you ship it with data that is prepopulated in the database that is used for the app. In our case, Quickstart has to populate a few items in the "to do list" table. This way, when you open the app, you will see some sample data. And in our new tables that we added in the preceding parts, we must populate the Questions table with some questions and some answers to select from, as this is required to make the app work. In this part, you will seed data for the database, and we will publish the app service.

1. For one-time initialization, open the `Startup.MobileApp.cs` file in the `App_Start` folder in Solution Explorer.

2. At about line 52, the `BookPollAppInitializer :CreateDatabaseIfNotExists<BookPollAppService>` database initializer class directs Entity Framework to create the database tables required to run the service, if no tables exist in the database. This initializer only runs once. If we later add/change/ delete a DTO, the service will throw an exception indicating that the schema is out of date and does not match the model.

Note   To re-create tables when a schema changes, you have to change the database initializer class to `DropCreateDatabaseIf ModelChanges<BookPollAppService>`, which instructs Entity Framework to drop all the tables and re-create them if the model (BookPollAppService) or any DTOs in the model change. Recall that when we add a new Table Controller, a `DbSet` property is created in the BookPollAppService to represent the table. The system identifies this using reflection and recognizes that the database schema is different. It will then re-create all the tables, using the current model; however, we will lose all our data. `DropCreateDatabaseAlways` will always drop the tables and create. Data must be migrated in these scenarios.

---

3. Keep `CreateDatabaseIfNotExists` on first run, then if you do subsequent runs, you can change to either `DropCreateDatabaseIfModelChanges` or `DropCreateDatabaseAlways`.

4. Replace the protected override void Seed method code with the following, which seeds data for the `TodoItem` list as well as PollQuestions (the source for `Startup.MobileApp.cs` is in the `Assets` folder, if you wish to copy the seed override method):

    ```
    public class BookPollAppInitializer :
    CreateDatabaseIfNotExists <BookPollAppContext>
    {
        protected override void Seed(BookPollAppContext
        context)
        {
    ```

```
List<TodoItem> todoItems = new
List<TodoItem>
{
    new TodoItem { Id = Guid.NewGuid().
    ToString(), Text = "First item",
    Complete = false },
    new TodoItem { Id = Guid.NewGuid().
    ToString(), Text = "Second item",
    Complete = false },
};

foreach (TodoItem todoItem in todoItems)
{
    context.Set<TodoItem>().Add(todoItem);
}
List<PollQuestion> Questions = new
List<PollQuestion>
{
    new PollQuestion { Id = Guid.NewGuid().
    ToString(), Text = "What book would you
    like to read?",
        Answers = "Beginning Entity
        Framework Core 2.0|Beginning
        Windows Mixed Reality
        Programming|Business in Real-Time,
        Using Azure IoT|Cyber Security on
        Azure|Angular 5 and .NET Core 2" },
    new PollQuestion { Id = Guid.NewGuid().
    ToString(), Text = "What is your
    favorite book category?",
```

```
            Answers = "Apple and iPS|Programming|
            Machine Learning|Mobile|Microsoft
            and .NET" },
    };
    foreach (PollQuestion question in Questions)
    {
        context.Set<PollQuestion>().
        Add(question);
    }
     context.SaveChanges();
    base.Seed(context);
  }
}
```

5. Your code should look like that shown in Figure 4-24.

```
13   namespace BookPollAppService
14   {
15       public partial class Startup
16       {
17           public static void ConfigureMobileApp(IAppBuilder app)
18           {
19               HttpConfiguration config = new HttpConfiguration();
20
21               //For more information on Web API tracing, see http://go.microsoft.com/fwlink/?LinkId=620686
22               config.EnableSystemDiagnosticsTracing();
23
24               new MobileAppConfiguration()
25                   .UseDefaultConfiguration()
26                   .ApplyTo(config);
27
28               // Use Entity Framework Code First to create database tables based on your DbContext
29               Database.SetInitializer(new BookPollAppInitializer());
30
31               // To prevent Entity Framework from modifying your database schema, use a null database initializer
32               // Database.SetInitializer<BookPollAppContext>(null);
33
34               MobileAppSettingsDictionary settings = config.GetMobileAppSettingsProvider().GetMobileAppSettings();
35
36               if (string.IsNullOrEmpty(settings.HostName))
37               {
38                   // This middleware is intended to be used locally for debugging. By default, HostName will
39                   // only have a value when running in an App Service application.
40                   app.UseAppServiceAuthentication(new AppServiceAuthenticationOptions
41                   {
42                       SigningKey = ConfigurationManager.AppSettings["SigningKey"],
43                       ValidAudiences = new[] { ConfigurationManager.AppSettings["ValidAudience"] },
44                       ValidIssuers = new[] { ConfigurationManager.AppSettings["ValidIssuer"] },
45                       TokenHandler = config.GetAppServiceTokenHandler()
46                   });
47               }
48               app.UseWebApi(config);
49           }
50       }
51
52       public class BookPollAppInitializer : CreateDatabaseIfNotExists<BookPollAppContext>
53       {
54           protected override void Seed(BookPollAppContext context)
55           {
56               List<TodoItem> todoItems = new List<TodoItem>
57               {
58                   new TodoItem { Id = Guid.NewGuid().ToString(), Text = "First item", Complete = false },
59                   new TodoItem { Id = Guid.NewGuid().ToString(), Text = "Second item", Complete = false },
60               };
61
62               foreach (TodoItem todoItem in todoItems)
63               {
64                   context.Set<TodoItem>().Add(todoItem);
65               }
66
67               List<PollQuestion> Questions = new List<PollQuestion>
68               {
69                   new PollQuestion { Id = Guid.NewGuid().ToString(), Text = "What book would you like to read?",
70                       Answers = "Beginning Entity Framework Core 2.0|Beginning Windows Mixed Reality Programming|Bu
71                   new PollQuestion { Id = Guid.NewGuid().ToString(), Text = "What is your favorite book category?",
72                       Answers = "Apple and iPS|Programming|Machine Learning|Mobile|Microsoft and .NET" },
73               };
74               foreach (PollQuestion question in Questions)
75               {
76                   context.Set<PollQuestion>().Add(question);
77               }
78               context.SaveChanges();
79               base.Seed(context);
80           }
81       }
```

Figure 4-24. *The completed* `Startup.MobileApp.cs` *file in the* `App_Start` *folder*

6. Build the app. Drum roll please! Right-click the
    solution, and now you can publish the app. See
    Figure 4-25.

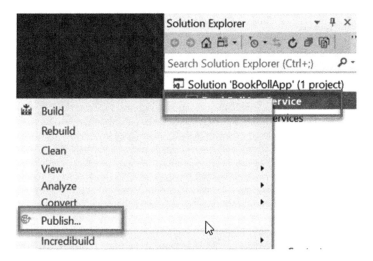

Figure 4-25. *Select the project, right-click, and select Publish... .*

7. Select Azure App Service, then Select Existing. See
    Figure 4-26.

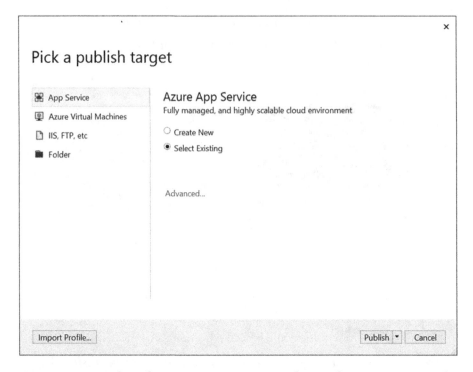

Figure 4-26. *Select the Azure App Service, then Select Existing, and click Publish... .*

8. Verify your credentials in the upper-right corner.
    Select your subscription and, under Resource
    Group, BookPollAppRG, then select your app
    service, BookPollApp. See Figure 4-27.

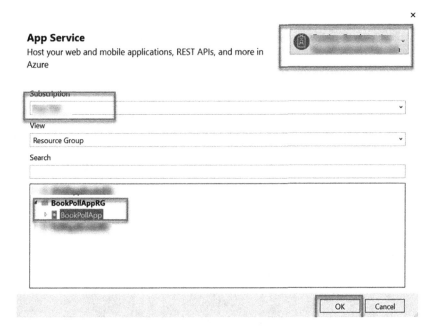

Figure 4-27. *Select your subscription and resource group from the drop-downs and select the app service you created in Quickstart under Resource Group*

9. The deployment should take a minute or two. Once deployed, you should see your browser pop up, with the service running as shown in Figure 4-28.

189

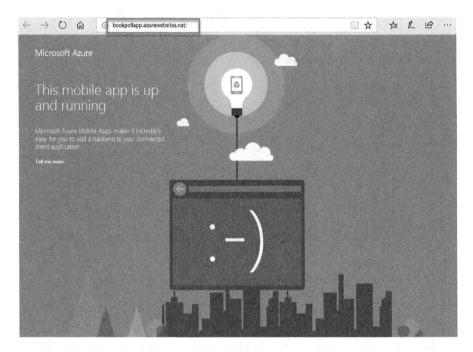

Figure 4-28. *Your web service should pop up in your browser, indicating that the mobile app is up and running!*

10. Now go back to the portal quick start and complete
     step 3, the final step, but only after you see that
     the web service is running. Click to download the
     Xamarin Forms client application for CREATE A
     NEW APP. See Figure 4-29. We will be connecting to
     an existing app in Chapter 5.

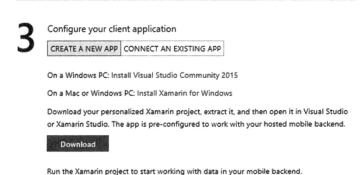

Figure 4-29. *Click the Download button to get your Xamarin Forms app, which is wired to your service and data*

Before you unzip, right-click the downloaded file and bring up the properties to unblock. Check Unblock and click OK. If you do not do this, you may encounter strange errors when running your app in Visual Studio. See Figure 4-30.

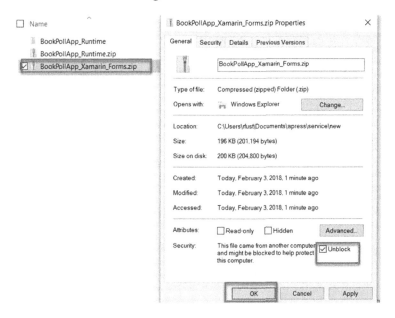

Figure 4-30. *Right-click the downloaded zip and select properties. Check Unblock and click OK.*

11. Right-click the solution and Restore NuGet
     Packages.

12. In the BookPollApp, open Constants.cs and verify
     that the application URL is set to what you created in
     Quickstart. See Figure 4-31.

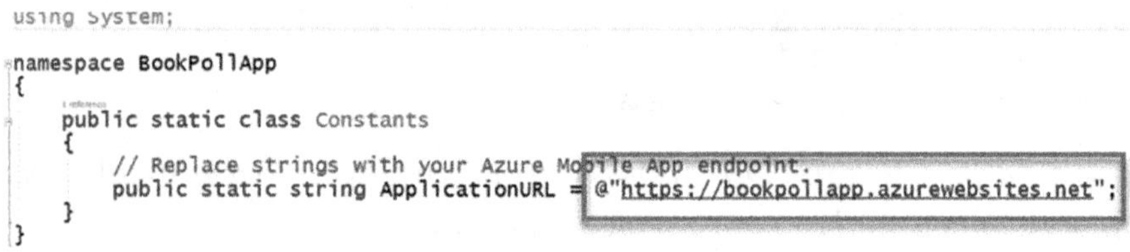

```
using System;

namespace BookPollApp
{
    public static class Constants
    {
        // Replace strings with your Azure Mobile App endpoint.
        public static string ApplicationURL = @"https://bookpollapp.azurewebsites.net";
    }
}
```

Figure 4-31. *Verify application URL in* Constants.cs

13. Right-click the UWP project and set as startup. See
     Figure 4-32.

Figure 4-32. *Right-click the UWP project and select Set as StartUp Project*

14. Rebuild the portable project and the UWP projects and any other platforms you wish to test.

15. **You need to run the app to populate the database tables.** For UWP, run the app on Local Machine ×86 or ×64 **(not ARM).** See Figure 4-33.

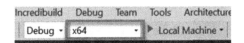

Figure 4-33. *Select ×64 or ×86 and then click Local Machine*

16. After the app starts, give it 5–10 seconds the first time, you should see a couple of "to do" items float into the list that were populated in the service app on our database. See Figure 4-34.

Figure 4-34. *See the "to-do list" items for the first and second items*

17. Go ahead and add a third entry. It will be stored in your Azure Database. See Figures 4-35 and 4-36.

Figure 4-35. *Add a third item to the list by typing a value and clicking +*

Figure 4-36. *You will see the third item added to the list*

Wow! That completes building your customized tables for an existing app and the table for the new app from Quickstart. We now have a working API that serves up data that our client apps can use. Are you feeling tingly yet? But wait...is the data really in the database? We know it is for the TodoItem table, because the preceding app shows it, but what about the Questions table? We need to verify this.

Part 6: Verify the Database

Time Estimate

10 Minutes

In this final part of the chapter, we will look at how to verify that the data has been seeded successfully in our application database. This is useful to do at this point, because in the next chapter, we must know if this part has been done correctly, or we will have data problems that are not in the app but in the database. So, we must eliminate that possibility. Let's accomplish this task and get started using SQL Server Management Studio.

Note You must run the Xamarin Forms app in Part 5, to see the data in Part 6. It does not seed tables in the database until used in the Xamarin Forms client app.

---

1. Go back to the portal and click Resource group on the left dashboard panel. Select BookPollAppRG, then select the SQL database, BookPollAppdb.

2. Copy the Database URL. See Figure 4-37.

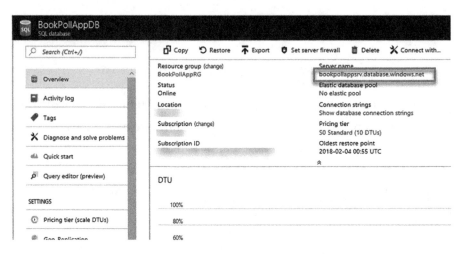

Figure 4-37. *Copy the server name URL for your database in the portal*

3. Start up SQL Server Management Studio, paste in the URL for the server name, and enter the login user and password that you set up for the database. Click Connect. See Figure 4-38.

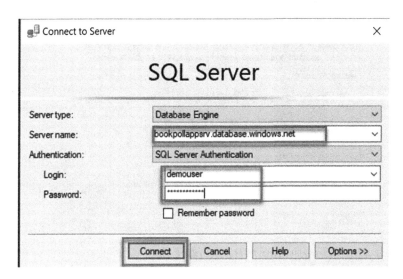

Figure 4-38. *Paste in the URL, enter the credentials you set up, and click Connect*

4. If you get prompted, sign in and create a new
    firewall rule. See Figures 4-39 and 4-40.

Figure 4-39. *Click Sign in and enter your credentials for the portal*

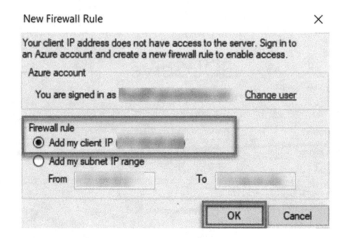

Figure 4-40. *Add my client IP and click OK*

5. Expand BookPollAppDB and Tables, right-click
   dbo.TodoItems, and click Select Top 1000 Rows.
   See Figure 4-41.

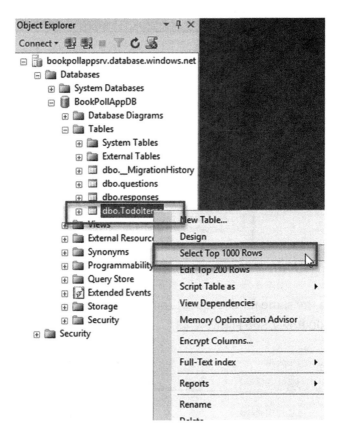

Figure 4-41. *Right-click* `dbo.TodoItems` *then click Select Top 1000 Rows*

6. You should see all three rows, including the one we
    added. See Figure 4-42.

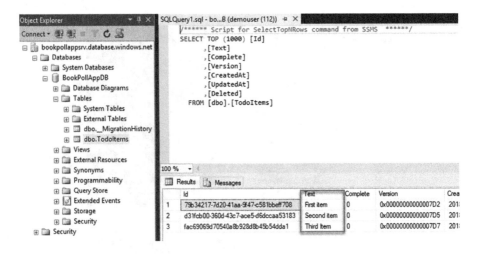

Figure 4-42. All three items are shown

7. Do the same for dbo.questions: click Select Top
    1000 Rows. See Figure 4-43.

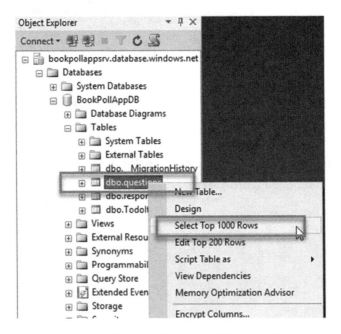

Figure 4-43. Select rows for the dbo.questions table

8. You should see the two questions we added. See
    Figure 4-44.

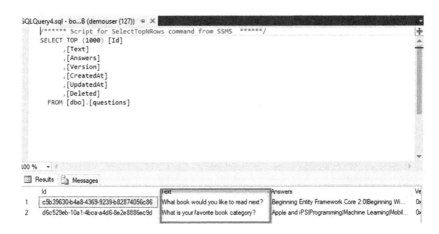

Figure 4-44. *Two questions should be displayed*

9. The Responses table will be empty. We will be
    populating that in Chapter 5.

10. You can also set up the firewall rules on the server.
    Navigate to the portal and open the database blade.
    Click Set server firewall. See Figure 4-45.

Figure 4-45. *You can set the server firewall on the portal as well*

11.   You should see the firewall rule that we just set up
       from SQL Server Management Studio. See Figure 4-46.

Figure 4-46. *The client IP we set up via SQL Server Management
Studio*

12.   Click on the + Add client IP to set up another one if
       you like. Click Save. Congratulations! You just built a
       service that can be consumed by any client. We will
       populate the Responses table and use the Questions
       table in the next chapter.

13. Type in the URLS to display the data in any current browser (except Internet Explorer, which will prompt you to download the results, which you can view with Notepad). Figure 4-47 shows the query for todoitem from the Edge browser. If you receive a message that resources have been moved or renamed, double-check the controller step 2 in Part 4, and make sure that you changed the name of the default controller from PollQuestionController to QuestionsController and did the same for responses.

```
[{"deleted":false,"updatedAt":"2018-02-19T18:52:04.368Z","createdAt":"2018-02-
19T18:52:04.352Z","version":"AAAAAAAAB9c=","id":"0b70f1a2-6276-4094-ae15-3d0f49ed4c48","complete":false,"text":"First item"},
{"deleted":false,"updatedAt":"2018-02-19T18:52:04.368Z","createdAt":"2018-02-
19T18:52:04.368Z","version":"AAAAAAAAB9o=","id":"4a5ebff4-cdfc-44c9-b0cb-6fddde86f4da","complete":false,"text":"Second item"}]
```

Figure 4-47. *The results for a query in a browser. This one is from Edge.*

From Firefox, query the Questions table, and it should appear nicely formatted, as in Figure 4-48. Enter the following URL: `https://bookpollapp. azurewebsites.net/tables/questions?ZUMO-API-VERSION=2.0.0`.

Figure 4-48. *The results for a query in a browser. These are from Firefox.*

203

14. Do not delete any resources from this chapter until you have completed Chapter 5.

Caution   Do not delete any resources from this chapter until you have completed Chapter 5.

Summary

In this chapter, you used the Azure portal to create a mobile app and Xamarin Forms' Quickstart to create a database for the app. Quickstart also created an app service using the Table API. You modified the Table API Service app and created two additional tables for questions and responses, which will be used in another Xamarin Forms app in Chapter 5. You have also seeded some data. You downloaded the sample Quickstart Xamarin Forms solution and ran it. You updated the "to do item" list and verified the database contents with SQL Server Management Studio and set up a server firewall rule.

In the next chapter, let's look at taking an existing Xamarin Forms app and integrating Azure, so we can consume the Questions table data that we exposed in our API app service. We will be populating the Responses table data in Chapter 5 from that same existing app. For the rest of the book, it is all about the client app!

CHAPTER 5

Building a Xamarin Forms Azure Client

When we used Quickstart in Chapter 4, we generated a new app that utilized Azure services. Now that you are liking Azure and, I hope, have seen the light, you may have an existing app that you would like to modify to use Azure. I have several apps that I have written for which I wish I had started using Azure from the get-go. This chapter will help you make modifications to an existing app and take advantage of the benefits that Azure has to offer. Something else that is often an afterthought is to make your app available and fully operational in an offline manner. The app we will be modifying in this chapter is fully functional from a local perspective, and we want to move the data for a local store to the cloud as well as synchronize it when offline. These are all common tasks many existing apps require today that cause headaches for developers.

In this chapter, you will modify an existing Xamarin Forms application to add support for utilizing an Azure mobile service. You can use any mix of the platform projects, depending on your development environment (Mac or Windows). You will customize data transfer objects (DTOs) and database query logic, as well as add offline caching support and synchronization.

© Russell Fustino 2018
R. Fustino, *Azure and Xamarin Forms*, https://doi.org/10.1007/978-1-4842-3561-4_5

Note   Run this project from your laptop/PC **and not an Azure Virtual Machine**. Chapter 4 must be completed, as it creates a service that will be consumed in Chapter 5. It creates an end point similar to `http://bookpollapp.azurewebsites.net`. Completed code for Chapter 4 is in this book's assets folder. The source code and assets for this book can be downloaded from `https://github.com/Apress/azure-and-xamarin-forms`.

The provided chapter 4 solution does not run and publish as is, It needs the Quickstart generated endpioint and Qucikstart generated configuration in Web.config as well as appropriate NuGet packages.

You must publish the app service in Chapter 4, exposing the end point similar to above.

We will not be using the Xamarin Client App created using Quickstart in Chapter 4. Instead, we will be using a starter project for Chapter 5. This chapter will provide knowledge on modifying an existing Xamarin Forms Client to "Azure-ize" it.

Time Estimate

65 Minutes

Part 1: Open an Existing Xamarin Forms Application

Time Estimate

5 Minutes

I have provided a fully functional app that works well with local data. The problem is that to make the app useful, the data really should be in the cloud, so the data is sharable among several users. Perhaps you have developed a prototype that runs local data and need to do that same thing. This is a very common problem in the developer community, for sure. The app provides questions with a list of choices for responses. Think of it as an app that facilitates polling or voting responses. In this part, you will be modifying an existing solution. You will open the starter solution, build it, run the project, and review the output.

1. Copy the Starter app from the book assets folder to a folder close to the root, such as `C:\Apressbooks`. From File Explorer, set properties to unblock and then unzip. With Visual Studio, open the Starter BookPollClientApp project.

2. As with any Xamarin Forms sample you download, always restore NuGet packages first. Right-click the solution and select Restore NuGet Packages. See Figure 5-1.

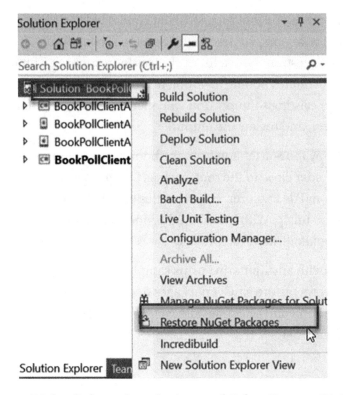

Figure 5-1. *Right click on the solution and Select Restore NuGet Packages*

3. Set the UWP project to the startup project. The next
    step is to build. Right-click the Portable project and
    select Build. See Figure 5-2.

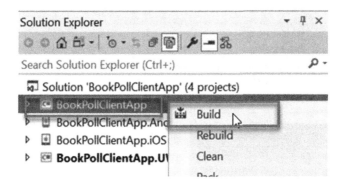

Figure 5-2. *Right-click the Portable and UWP projects and select*
Build

4. If you see errors in the Portable project related to
    EmbeddedResources, or other extraneous errors, do
    the following:

    • Right-click the project in the solution.

    • Unload the project.

    • Reload the project.

    • Build the project.

    This is another common problem on downloaded
    Xamarin samples. Sometimes you may also have to
    clean the solution (by right-clicking the solution),
    then delete the obj and bin folders by clicking the
    Show All Files button for each project. See
    Figures 5-3 through 5-6.

Figure 5-3. *An EmbeddedResource error is not really an error*

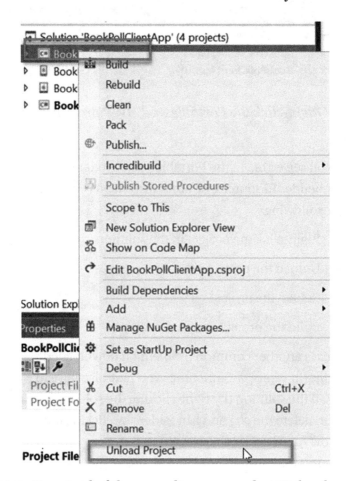

Figure 5-4. *To get rid of the preceding error, select Unload Project*

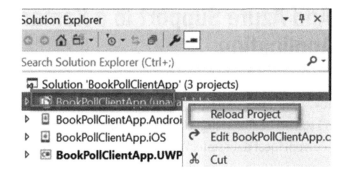

Figure 5-5. *By selecting Reload Project, the project should rebuild*

To resolve extraneous errors, sometimes you must clean project and delete the `bin` and `obj` folders. To see them, click the Show All Files button in Solution Explorer.

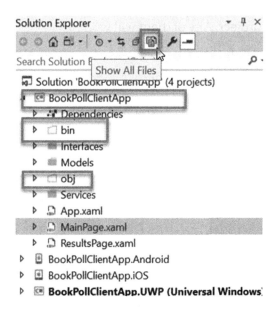

Figure 5-6. *Show All Files button in Solution Explorer*

Now we have a project that builds. Next, let's run it and see the application that currently runs from local data.

Part 2: Add Azure Support to a Xamarin Forms Application

Time Estimate

15 Minutes

Where do I start? The first thing will be to simply run the app and see it execute in its current local data state. We will review the structure of the app, so that you become a little more familiar with it. Then we will look at adding the appropriate NuGet packages that are required to access Azure Services. We will add the appropriate Azure initialization calls and create a PollQuestion interface. In this part, you will add Azure support to an existing application.

1. Continue with the same project.

2. Set your preferred platform-specific project as the startup project. Any of them will work.

3. Run the application to see it work. See Figure 5-7.

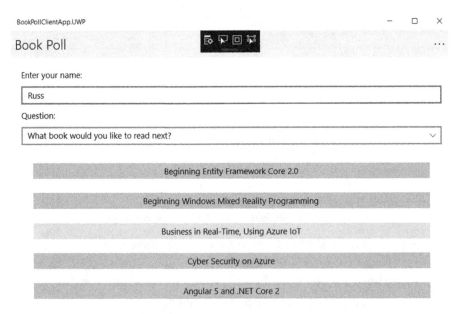

Figure 5-7. *Running the starter app should look like this*

4. Expand the solution—it contains several projects, as listed in Table 5-1.

Table 5-1. *Solution Project Layout*

Project	Description
BookPollClientApp	This is the core Xamarin.Forms view shared assembly. It contains the page definitions (one for the main page and one for a results page), the models, and the code that will interact with the service. Currently, it has a mocked-out implementation that does everything with hard-coded local data. You will be using the IPollQuestionService interface, which you will implement to connect to Azure Service.
BookPollClientApp.Android	The Xamarin.Android platform-specific (head) project
BookPollClientApp.iOS	The Xamarin.iOS platform-specific (head) project. You will require a Mac host to run this application.
BookPollClientApp.UWP	The Windows UWP platform-specific (head) project. You will require Visual Studio for Windows to run this project. It will be disabled on macOS.

5. We need the Azure client libraries in our projects and to add NuGet references. This will allow us to connect to Azure and interact with the exposed table end points. Add the Microsoft.Azure.Mobile. Client NuGet package to all of the projects. Right-click the solution and select Manage NuGet Packages for Solution… . Click the browse tab and search on Microsoft.Azure.Mobile.Client. Check all the projects, as shown in Figure 5-8.

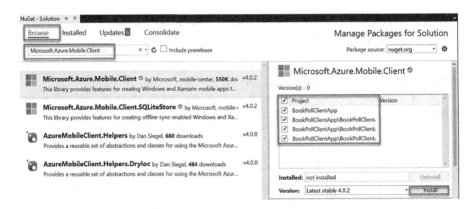

Figure 5-8. Browse for Microsoft.Azure.Mobile.Client and install to all the projects

6. If you see errors in the Error list after loading the mobile client, click Save All and close and reopen Visual Studio with the project.

7. Next, we must initialize the Azure library. Both Android and iOS must initialize the Azure client library, by adding a line of code into the initialization of the app. This code must be done in the platform-specific projects, as the method isn't available in the shared project. You only have to do this for Android and iOS—and only if you plan to run these platforms.

8. For Android, open the `MainActivity.cs` file in the Xamarin.Android project. Because this is a Xamarin. Forms app, the main Activity only launches once per app-launch, and we can do our initialization here.

9. Add a call to `Microsoft.WindowsAzure.`
   `MobileServices.CurrentPlatform.Init();` in the
   `OnCreate` override. You can place it just before the
   `Forms.Init` call. The following highlighted code is
   what you must add:

```
protected override void OnCreate(Bundle bundle)
{
    TabLayoutResource = Resource.Layout.Tabbar;
    ToolbarResource = Resource.Layout.Toolbar;

    base.OnCreate(bundle);
    Microsoft.WindowsAzure.MobileServices.
    CurrentPlatform.Init();

    global::Xamarin.Forms.Forms.Init(this, bundle);
    LoadApplication(new App());
}
```

10. For iOS, open the `AppDelegate.cs` file in the
    Xamarin.iOS project.

11. Add a call to `Microsoft.WindowsAzure.`
    `MobileServices.CurrentPlatform.Init ();` in the
    `FinishedLaunching` override. You can place it just
    before the `Forms.Init` call.

```
public override bool FinishedLaunching(UIApplication
app, NSDictionary options)
        {
            Microsoft.WindowsAzure.MobileServices.
            CurrentPlatform.Init();
            global::Xamarin.Forms.Forms.Init();
```

```
                    LoadApplication(new App());

                    return base.FinishedLaunching(app,
                    options);
            }
```

12. Let's create a new service class to interact with Azure. The interface is defined to interact with our poll data service. Currently, it's implemented with a mock class for local testing. Our goal is to eventually replace this with a complete implementation that talks to Azure (or some other online cloud provider). Open the IPollQuestionService.cs file in the Interfaces folder of the BookPollClientApp project. This is the interface we must implement.

13. Let's start by creating a new class that implements the interface. Add a new class named AzurePollService.cs in the Services folder.

14. Make the class public, and have it implement IPollQuestionService. You can use the built-in IDE support to add each required method stub. We won't actually be providing an implementation yet, but all the methods must be present. Just leave the throw new NotImplementedException(); in place for now. Add these using statements:

using BookPollClientApp.Interfaces;
using Microsoft.WindowsAzure.MobileServices;

15. Make the class public, and as you type in the interface to inherit, you should see the Intellisense show the IPollQuestionService interface. See Figure 5-9.

```
using System;
using System.Collections.Generic;
using System.Text;
using BookPollClientApp.Interfaces;

namespace BookPollClientApp.Interfaces
{
    public class AzurePollService : Ip
        interface BookPollClientApp.Interfaces.IPollQuestionService
    }
}
```

Figure 5-9. *Select the Intellisense for IPollQuestionService*

16. Hover over the red squiggle on IPollQuestionService
     and select the Show potential fixes icon. Select
     Implement interface. See Figure 5-10.

Figure 5-10. *Select Implement interface*

17. To interact with Azure Service, you use a
     MobileServiceClient object. We'll create one and
     place it into our new AzurePollService class. Add a
     new private field of type MobileServiceClient. Add
     a new private method named Initialize, create

217

a mobile service client object, and assign it to your field. You will require the URL of the Azure service to pass into the constructor. We are working with a pre-built service from Chapter 4. The URL to the pre-built server from Chapter 4 is similar to http://bookpollapp.azurewebsites.net.

Add this using statement to AzurePollService.cs and the following code:

```
using Microsoft.WindowsAzure.MobileServices;

public class AzurePollService : IPollQuestionService
    {
        const string AzureUrl = @"http://bookpollapp.
        azurewebsites.net";
        MobileServiceClient client;
        void Initialize()
        {
            client = new MobileServiceClient(AzureUrl);
        }

        public Task AddOrUpdatePollResponseAsync(PollRe
        sponse response)
        {
            throw new NotImplementedException();
        }
    ...
```

18. Add a check into the Initialize method, to see if the MobileServiceClient has been created (non-null) and, if so, return. We want to be able to call this method multiple times but have the logic executed only once.

19. Next, add a call to the Initialize method into **each**
    of your implementation methods. We will create it
    the first time we use the object (as opposed to when
    it is created).

```
public class AzurePollService :
IPollQuestionService
{
    const string AzureUrl = "http://bookpollapp.
    azurewebsites.net";
    MobileServiceClient client;
    void Initialize()
    {
        if (client != null)
            return;
        client = new MobileServiceClient(AzureUrl);
    }
    public Task AddOrUpdatePollResponseAsync
    (PollResponse response)
    {
        Initialize();
        throw new NotImplementedException();
    }
    public Task DeletePollResponseAsync
    (PollResponse response)
    {
        Initialize();
        throw new NotImplementedException();
    }
    ...
```

20. Now, let's use our new Azure service and replace the service mock! Open the `MainPage.xaml. cs` file in the Portable project. It allocates an `IPollQuestionService` as a field in the class. Replace the `MockPollQuestionService` instance with a new `AzurePollService` instance.

```
public partial class MainPage : ContentPage
{
    // TODO: replace implementation
    readonly IPollQuestionService service = new
    AzurePollService();
```

21. Run the application. It should now fail and display a message indicating that the called method is not implemented. However, we will have created our Azure connection and are now set up to start implementing data access methods! See Figure 5-11.

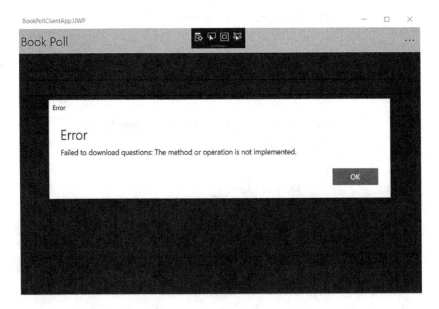

Figure 5-11. *Run, and an expected error will occur*

Congrats! You have started the journey to add Azure services to your app. Let's proceed to the next step and get the app to be functional again, by customizing the DTOs for the polling service.

Part 3: Customize the DTOs for the Polling Service

Time Estimate

10 Minutes

What we must do is wire the data we created in Chapter 4, now in the cloud, to the app. The plumbing is done thru DTOs, as we saw in Chapter 4 when serving up the data. Here, we will be using the DTOs to consume the data. Also, the data coming across the wire may have slightly different names than we are using in our app. No problem. That's what JSON attributes are for. Just specify the name of the field you are getting from the service in the attribute, and it will map it automatically for you. Phew! No major renaming in my app! In this part, you will customize the DTOs by adding `Json` and `Table` attributes.

There are two classes defined in the app that are used to hold the data that drives the user interface (UI):

> `PollQuestion`: This class holds a single question that includes text and a set of answers delimited by a "|".

> `PollResponse`: This class is used to represent the response to a poll question. It includes a property for the responder's name, the question ID being answered, and the index of the answer chosen.

The server end points we will be interacting with have data similar to the preceding data structures; however, when the developers created the service, they deviated slightly from the specification (or maybe we deviated from the specification when creating the client!).

The two classes will require Json.NET attributes, to set the name of the table. Make sure the properties conform to the preceding data structures.

We have to modify the DTO to match the JSON response. If we tried to use the current data structures as DTOs, they would not map much of the API, and, in fact, would actually hit the wrong end point, for example, PollQuestion instead of questions. We could fix this by renaming the class and its properties, but that's undesirable, because it would ripple throughout the application. Instead, let's fix this problem by applying Json.NET attributes to our DTO, to change the serialization format.

1. Open the PollQuestion.cs source file in the Models folder.

   Note that the property names don't match our JSON-expected shape, and the name of the class is being used as the end point name, which doesn't match.

2. Add a [Newtonsoft.Json.JsonObject(Title="questions")] attribute to the class, to fix the end point name. Add the following using statement and code:

```
using Newtonsoft.Json;

namespace BookPollClientApp.Models
{
    [JsonObject(Title = "questions")]
    public class PollQuestion
    {
        public string Id { get; set; }

        public string Text { get; set; }
        public string Answers { get; set; }
```

```
        public override string ToString()
        {
            return Text;
        }
    }
}
```

3. Do the same fix for the `PollResponse` object. Recall that the JSON shape

   • Is exposed on an end point named `"responses"`.

   • Has the fields `"questionId"`, `"name"`, and `"answer"`.

4. We will want to use the `createdAt` property a bit later, so add a new property to provide access to the field.

```
using Newtonsoft.Json;
using Microsoft.WindowsAzure.MobileServices;
using System;

namespace BookPollClientApp.Models
{
    [JsonObject(Title = "responses")]
    public class PollResponse
    {
        public string Id { get; set; }
        [JsonProperty("questionId")]
        public string PollQuestionId { get; set; }
        public string Name { get; set; }
        [JsonProperty("answer")]
        public int ResponseIndex { get; set; }
```

```
            [UpdatedAt]
            public DateTimeOffset UpdatedAt { get; set; }


        }
    }
```

Looks like our data structures are now intact. But how about the logic methods to work with our data?

Part 4: Fill In the Logic to Query and Update Our Poll Records

Time Estimate

10 Minutes

Data is useless unless we can get at it and pull it into the app. We may want to have methods to pull back all the questions. Perhaps we want to pull back a specific question or perform an update or insert in a record set. In this part, you will provide the logic for database queries. Basically, we want to be able to perform create, read, update, and delete (CRUD) operations, using lists and/or individual records.

Now let's add support to query and update our created tables in the Azure service we created.

- Implement the GetQuestionsAsync method, which retrieves all the questions from the questions table.

- Implement the GetResponseForPollAsync method, which retrieves a single response record.

- Implement the GetResponsesForPollAsync method, which retrieves all response records.

- Implement the `AddOrUpdatePollResponseAsync` method, to add or update the passed record, based on whether it exists in the database.

- Finally, implement the `DeletePollResponseAsync` method, to remove an existing poll response.

1. Let's create a table accessor for the questions table. We have to retrieve an IMobileServiceTable implementation for the questions. Luckily, we already have a DTO defined in the `Models` folder of our data project, which we just updated to support the proper schema.

2. Open `AzurePollService.cs`. In the `Initialize` method of your service, make a call to the mobile service client `GetTable` method using `PollQuestion` as the DTO. This will return `IMobileServiceT` `able<PollQuestion>`, which you should store in a class field (the chapter names this field `"questionsTable"`).

```
public class AzurePollService : IPollQuestionService
{
    const string AzureUrl = @"http://bookpollapp.
    azurewebsites.net";
    MobileServiceClient client;
    IMobileServiceTable<PollResponse>
    responseTable;
    IMobileServiceTable<PollQuestion>
    questionsTable;
    void Initialize()
    {
```

```
            if (client != null)
                return;
            client = new MobileServiceClient(AzureUrl);
            questionsTable = client.
            GetTable<PollQuestion>();
            responseTable = client.
            GetTable<PollResponse>();
    }
```

3. Next, to read all the questions, use the table
    interface and implement the GetQuestionsAsync
    method for your service. This just returns
    Task<IEnumerable<PollQuestion>>, which
    matches nicely with one of the retrieval methods
    discussed in the class.

```
        public Task<IEnumerable<PollQuestion>>
        GetQuestionsAsync()
        {
            Initialize();
            return questionsTable.ReadAsync();
        }
```

4. Run the application and verify that questions show
    up from Azure. (Do not try to type a name in yet or
    you will get an error - we will fix this) One method
    down! See Figure 5-12.

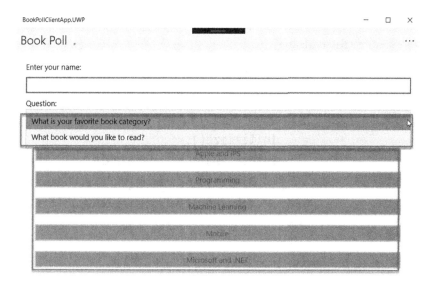

Figure 5-12. *The questions have been populated and connected to Azure*

5. Next, let's work with the responses table. The steps here are pretty much identical to those we performed with questions. Use the table interface to retrieve the top 100 responses, to implement the GetResponsesForPollAsync method for your service. Order the data by the CreatedAt property in descending order. The method we are modifying here for GetResponsesForPollAsync only has one parameter, questionId (not to be confused with the method called GetResponseForPollAsync, which has two parameters).

- Order the data by the CreatedAt property in descending order.

- Restrict the query to 100 records with the Take method.

- You will need to add a ToEnumerableAsync method to the call.

```
public async Task<IEnumerable<PollResponse>>
GetResponsesForPollAsync(string questionId)
{
    Initialize();
    return await responseTable
        .OrderByDescending(r => r.UpdatedAt)
        .Take(100).ToEnumerableAsync();
}
```

6. Next, implement the GetResponseForPollAsync
    method, by adding a Where clause to the table.
    Implement the following code to return the
    first PollResponse result from the Enumerable
    collection that matches the questionId and the
    name parameters. Also, you will have to add a using
    statement for System.Linq.

```
using System.Linq;
```

```
public async Task<PollResponse>
GetResponseForPollAsync(string questionId,
string name)
{
    Initialize();
    return (await responseTable.Where(r =>
    r.PollQuestionId == questionId &&
    r.Name == name)
.ToEnumerableAsync()).FirstOrDefault();
}
```

7. Implement the DeletePollResponseAsync method, using the table DeleteAsync method. This is a straight call. You will have to use async and await in this method.

```
public async Task DeletePollResponseAsync(PollR
esponse response)
{
 Initialize();
 await responseTable.DeleteAsync(response);
}
```

8. Finally, implement the AddOrUpdatePollResponseAsync method. You will either have to call InsertAsync or UpdateAsync, based on whether the request is in the database. You can tell if the value already exists in the database by looking at the Id property. If it's null or empty, it's a new response.

```
public Task AddOrUpdatePollResponseAsync(PollRe
sponse response)
{
    Initialize();
    if (string.IsNullOrEmpty(response.Id))
    {
        return responseTable.
        InsertAsync(response);
    }
    return responseTable.UpdateAsync(response);
}
```

9. Run the app again. We now have a complete
    implementation, and it should work exactly the
    way it did with your local mocked service, except
    now, the data is persisted. If you run this on
    different devices, you'll see the same data shared
    across them, because it's stored in the cloud! Click
    the menu to see your responses or delete them. See
    Figures 5-13 and 5-14. We have made quite a few
    changes to the current project and the completed
    project through Part 4 of Chapter 5 is located in this
    book's assets folder, in case you have to double-check
    your work.

Note   The source code and assets for this book can be downloaded
from `https://github.com/Apress/azure-and-xamarin-forms`

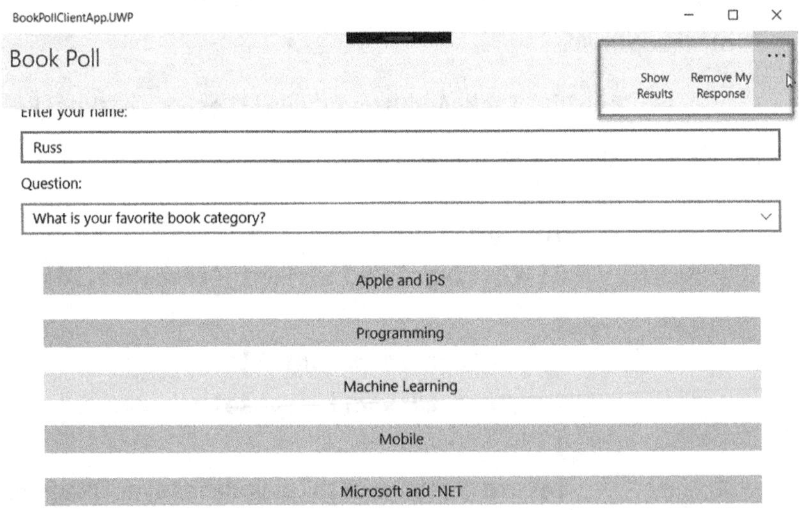

Figure 5-13. *Select the menu choice for Show Results, after clicking
on an answer and entering your name*

Figure 5-14. *See the list of poll answers and enter more*

Wow! We now have a functioning app that is using cloud-based data. Congrats! You may want to save this project, so that you can come back to it, if needed, when working on this chapter's next part, on adding offline caching to the app. You are at a good checkpoint.

Part 5: Add Support to Our App for Offline Data Caching

Time Estimate

15 Minutes

Many apps today require an offline strategy. For example, say you have an app that works in the field for an electric company, and you need to have it work all the time, even in rural areas where Internet and cellular connectivity is poor. Well, this is a perfect reason to store the updates and retrieve copies of the data locally. Once connectivity is restored, you can update the cloud data. I always thought this was a tough nut to crack, before I learned Azure, but you will be amazed at how simple this is, using SQLite for local storage and Azure services for synchronization. In this part, you will add support for offline caching, using SQLite.

- Add the Microsoft.Azure.Mobile.Client.SQLiteStore NuGet package to all the projects.

- Add the required SQLite PCL initialization code into the iOS head/platform project.

- Create a new MobileServiceSQLiteStore to hold our local data.

- Define our two tables in the SQLite store.

- Initialize `MobileServiceClient.SyncContext` with the SQLite store.

- Change the table definitions to use `IMobileServiceSyncTable`.

- To add support offline caching, we must add a reference to another NuGet package and call an initialize method for our iOS application, as follows:

1. Add a NuGet reference to the Microsoft.Azure. Mobile.Client.SQLiteStore package to each of the platform-specific (head) projects and to your PCL. See Figure 5-15.

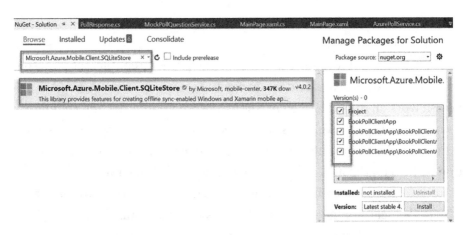

Figure 5-15. *Add the NuGet package for Microsoft.Azure.Mobile. Client.SQLiteStore to all projects.*

2. Next, in the iOS platform-specific project, open
    AppDelegate.cs and add a call to SQLitePCL.
    CurrentPlatform.Init ();, to initialize the SQLite-
    managed library. This should happen as part of your
    application initialization, just as when initializing
    the Azure client library. This is only required for
    iOS. You may have to add another NuGet package
    SQLitePCL by Microsoft Open Technologies. See
    Figure 5-16.

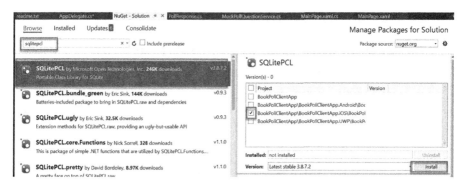

Figure 5-16. *Add NuGet package for SQLitePCL to the iOS project*

```
public override bool FinishedLaunching(UIApplication
app, NSDictionary options)
{
    Microsoft.WindowsAzure.MobileServices.
    CurrentPlatform.Init();
    SQLitePCL.CurrentPlatform.Init();
    global::Xamarin.Forms.Forms.Init();
    LoadApplication(new App());
    return base.FinishedLaunching(app, options);
}
```

3. Next, we have to initialize our local database, so
   the Azure client can work with a local data source,
   instead of the remote database.

4. Open your AzurePollService.cs service you have
   been working on.

5. In the Initialize method, create a new
   MobileServiceSQLiteStore and store it in a local field
   in the method.

6. Next, call a DefineTable<T> method on the database
   store for our two DTOs.

using Microsoft.WindowsAzure.MobileServices.
SQLiteStore;

• • •

```
      void Initialize()
      {
          if (client != null)
              return;
          var store = new
          MobileServiceSQLiteStore("Poll.db");
          store.DefineTable<PollQuestion>();
          store.DefineTable<PollResponse>();

          client = new MobileServiceClient(AzureUrl);
          questionsTable = client.
          GetTable<PollQuestion>();
          responseTable = client.
          GetTable<PollResponse>();
      }
```

7. The location for `poll.db` will be in the appropriate
    app storage area for the platform. For example, in
    Windows, you will see it at the following location,
    after we run the app: `C:\Users\{user}\AppData\`
    `Local\Packages\{long guid}\LocalState`.

8. Uninstalling the app in any platform will also
    uninstall the local database, as it is part of the app
    deployment.

9. When using SQLite, we must use all data-
    related methods as `Async` methods, or your app
    might crash. Next, call the `InitializeAsync`
    method on the `SyncContext` property of your
    `MobileServiceClient`.

    •   Pass the created store as the first parameter.

    •   Pass a new instance of a
        `MobileServiceSyncHandler` object as the second
        parameter. This class is what executes the async
        calls to synchronize the database. We are using the
        default implementation.

10. Note that this method is asynchronous and returns
    a `Task`. To make this easier to work with, you can
    modify the method to be async and return a `Task`, so
    errors propagate out.

11.   Rename the method to InitializeAsync, so it is
clear that this method is asynchronous. You can use
the Rename refactoring, to ensure this change goes
through the class. Use this using statement and the
code below.

```
using Microsoft.WindowsAzure.MobileServices.Sync;

        async Task InitializeAsync()
        {
            if (client != null)
                return;
            var store = new
            MobileServiceSQLiteStore("Poll.db");
            store.DefineTable<PollQuestion>();
            store.DefineTable<PollResponse>();

            client = new MobileServiceClient(AzureUrl);

            await client.SyncContext.
            InitializeAsync(store, new
            MobileServiceSyncHandler());

    . . .

        }
```

12. That last change ripples throughout our class, because we call InitializeAsync from every method. Fix all the methods, using the await keyword on each call to InitializeAsync. You can use the following code as a guide, to apply the keywords into the correct place, if you need some help:

```
public async Task AddOrUpdatePollResponseAsync(
PollResponse response)
{
   await InitializeAsync();
    if (string.IsNullOrEmpty(response.Id))
    {
        await responseTable.
        InsertAsync(response);
    }
    await responseTable.UpdateAsync(response);
}

public async Task<IEnumerable<PollQuestion>>
GetQuestionsAsync()
{
    await InitializeAsync();
    return await questionsTable.ReadAsync();
}
public async Task<PollResponse>
GetResponseForPollAsync(string questionId,
string name)
{
    await InitializeAsync();
    return (await responseTable.Where(r =>
    r.PollQuestionId == questionId && r.Name
    == name)
```

237

```csharp
        .ToEnumerableAsync()).FirstOrDefault();
    }
    public async Task<IEnumerable<PollResponse>>
    GetResponsesForPollAsync(string questionId)
    {
        await InitializeAsync();
        return await responseTable
          .OrderByDescending(r => r.UpdatedAt)
          .Take(100).ToEnumerableAsync();
    }
    public async Task DeletePollResponseAsync(PollR
    esponse response)
    {
        await InitializeAsync();
        await responseTable.DeleteAsync(response);
    }
```

13. The final step in switching to our local cache is to use the IMobileServiceSyncTable interface instead of our normal IMobileServiceTable.

14. Change the two fields holding the questions and responses to be IMobileServiceSyncTable.

15. Change the call to GetTable on the MobileServiceClient> to GetSyncTable.

```csharp
            const string AzureUrl = "http://
            bookpollapp.azurewebsites.net";
MobileServiceClient client;
IMobileServiceSyncTable<PollQuestion>
questionsTable;
IMobileServiceSyncTable<PollResponse>
responseTable;
```

```
async Task InitializeAsync()
{
    if (client != null)
        return;
    var store = new
    MobileServiceSQLiteStore("Poll.db");
    store.DefineTable<PollQuestion>();
    store.DefineTable<PollResponse>();

    client = new MobileServiceClient(AzureUrl);

    await client.SyncContext.
    InitializeAsync(store, new
    MobileServiceSyncHandler());
    questionsTable = client.
    GetSyncTable<PollQuestion>();
    responseTable = client.
    GetSyncTable<PollResponse>();

}
```

16. Run the application to see the results. If you get an
    error such as "The specified path, file name or both,"
    close the project, shorten the folder names, reopen,
    rebuild, and run the application again. You can also
    simply copy the entire project closer to the root of
    your drive, as another alternative.

17. We are now using our local cached data—except we
    have no data! So, the screen will come up without
    data. The next step is to learn how to synchronize
    our data to the remote database.

I can see light at the end of the tunnel. Can you? We are building things to a crescendo, to the most exciting part in this chapter: synchronization. It will take your app to a professional level.

Part 6: Synchronizing to the Remote Database

Time Estimate

10 Minutes

Not only will you add and learn the code that does the magic on synchronization, you will also learn to use some tools to see what is going across the wire. When I presented this at a recent Azure Developer Event, the crowd went wild! Really. In this part, you will test offline use and synchronization.

- Use Edge, Firefox, or Chrome to query the data. (Internet Explorer will not display but makes available the results via a downloaded file.)

- You can also use Postman to query the data.

- Push any changes to the remote database when the app is launched.

- Pull down the latest questions table when the app is launched.

- Synchronize changes to the responses table each time we change the question or the name.

1. Because you'll now be working offline, it's helpful to be able to look at what's currently on the server. You can do this by hitting the responses table directly with a REST client, such as Postman or Edge, Chrome or Firefox. The end point you want to GET is `https://bookpollapp.azurewebsites.net/tables/responses`, and use the header for ZUMO-API-VERSION with the value 2.0.0.

2. Let's use Firefox, as it formats the data that is displayed. As the URL, type `https://bookpollapp.azurewebsites.net/tables/responses?ZUMO-API-VERSION=2.0.0`. See Figure 5-17.

Figure 5-17. *Firefox display of table responses*

3. Let's start by synchronizing the questions table.
    We'll do this as part of our initialization logic in our
    service code. Locate the `InitializeAsync` method
    and use the `MobileServiceClient.SyncContext`
    to push changes to the remote database after we
    initialize our sync tables. After you've pushed
    changes that may have been made while offline, go
    ahead and pull all questions down. Because these
    don't change frequently, we'll just pull them down
    once, as part of our initialization code. Because this
    is part of our initialization code, go ahead and pass
    in a query name (such as `"allQuestions"`), so we
    turn on incremental sync. You can use a standard
    full query. Make sure to catch exceptions. For now,
    just dump the exception to the debug console, using
    `Debug.WriteLine`. Run the app and verify that you
    get questions in the UI now. Use the following using
    statement and code:

using System.Diagnostics;

```
async Task InitializeAsync()
{
    if (client != null)
        return;
    var store = new
    MobileServiceSQLiteStore("Poll.db");
    store.DefineTable<PollQuestion>();
    store.DefineTable<PollResponse>();

    client = new MobileServiceClient(AzureUrl);
```

```
await client.SyncContext.
InitializeAsync(store, new
MobileServiceSyncHandler());
questionsTable = client.
GetSyncTable<PollQuestion>();
responseTable = client.GetSyncTable<PollRe
sponse>();
try
{
    await client.SyncContext.PushAsync();
    await questionsTable.PullAsync(
        "allQuestions", questionsTable.
        CreateQuery());
}
catch (Exception ex)
{
    Debug.WriteLine("Got exception: {0}",
    ex.Message);
}
}
```

4. Next, we must write a method to synchronize our
    response table. Because this table will be changed
    by our app (and on the server), we will have to
    synchronize it more often than the questions.
    Because the app always works with responses only
    for the current question, we'll use a custom query
    that only synchronizes for a specific question.
    Add a new method, SynchronizeResponsesAsync,
    that returns a Task and takes a string that is the
    questionId we want to retrieve responses for.
    Use the PullAsync method to retrieve only the

responses for the passed questionId. We can turn on incremental sync by supplying a query name. However, it must be unique for each query, meaning it has to take into account the questionId. The easiest way to do that is to generate a unique string by appending the questionId itself. As with the previous code, make sure to catch exceptions. Just output them to the debug console.

```
async Task SynchronizeResponsesAsync(string
questionId)
{
    try
    {
        await responseTable.
        PullAsync("syncResponses" + questionId,
                        responseTable.Where(
                        r => r.PollQuestionId
                        == questionId));
    }
    catch (Exception ex)
    {
        // TODO: handle error
        Debug.WriteLine("Got exception: {0}",
        ex.Message);
    }
}
```

5. We will want to perform the response
    synchronization each time we change a record, so
    add a call to our new SynchronizeResponsesAsync
    method into your AddOrUpdatePollResponseAsync
    and DeletePollResponseAsync methods after you
    make the change.

```
public async Task AddOrUpdatePollResponseAsync(
PollResponse response)
{
    await InitializeAsync();
    if (string.IsNullOrEmpty(response.Id))
    {
        await responseTable.
        InsertAsync(response);
    }
    await responseTable.UpdateAsync(response);
    await SynchronizeResponsesAsync(response.
    PollQuestionId);
}

public async Task DeletePollResponseAsync(PollR
esponse response)
{
    await InitializeAsync();
    await responseTable.DeleteAsync(response);
    await SynchronizeResponsesAsync(response.
    PollQuestionId);
}
```

6. We also want to synchronize to the response
    table when we change the current question
    or the name. In both cases, this will call our
    GetResponseForPollAsync method. However, we
    don't want to refresh against the table every single
    time because this is called quite often. Instead, let's
    only refresh if the passed questionId parameter
    changes.

    - Create a private field in the class to hold the last
      known questionId we refreshed our responses for.

    - Check the field against the passed questionId
      parameter. If it's different, then synchronize against
      the responses table using our method and set the
      last questionId field. Run the application, try
      adding and deleting a few records, and compare it
      to the online version through the REST client.

```
string lastQuestionId;
public async Task<PollResponse>
GetResponseForPollAsync(string questionId,
string name)
{
    await InitializeAsync();
    if (lastQuestionId != questionId)
    {
        // Get the latest responses for this
        // question.
        await SynchronizeResponsesAsync
        (questionId);
        lastQuestionId = questionId;
    }
```

```
      return (await responseTable.Where(r =>
      r.PollQuestionId == questionId && r.Name ==
      name)
  .ToEnumerableAsync()).FirstOrDefault();

    }
```

7. Run the app once, to cache the questions and responses.

8. Next, let's force the app offline and see how it responds. Prior to our changes, it would have simply failed. We have several ways we can test no network. If you are on a physical device, you can switch to Airplane mode. On a simulator, we can simply change the AzureUrl value to something we cannot resolve.

9. Change the AzureUrl constant string to be invalid. For example, change the ".net" suffix to ".zzz" (kind of like it's sawing wood!).

10. Run the application and make some changes offline. See Figure 5-18.

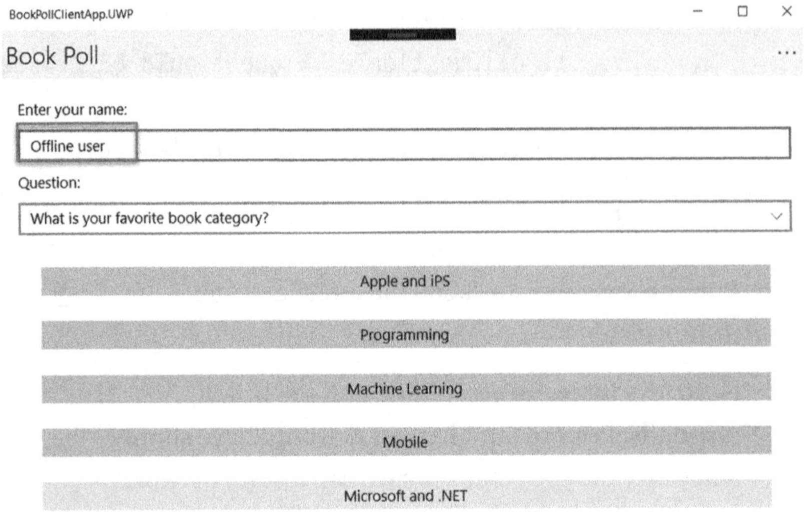

Figure 5-18. *Enter an offline user and select a book*

11. Shut down the app, reset the URL back, and run it
     again. When it launches, verify that your changes
     are still in the app, by looking at all responses. They
     should immediately synchronize back to the server.
     See Figure 5-19.

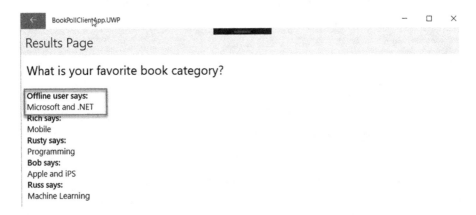

Figure 5-19. *Your offline entry should immediately synchronize back
to the server. Cool, huh? It's just that easy to sync.*

Summary

In this chapter, you added support to an existing Xamarin.Forms application to access an Azure mobile service. You finished the Xamarin client application and implemented a complete client to access the Azure Poll service and the main logic for the Xamarin client application. You added full support for locally caching data, using the built-in support. Finally, you completed your offline caching, by synchronizing your local database with the remote database on Azure.

CHAPTER 6

Delete Resources in Your Subscription

In this short chapter, you will delete the resource groups in your subscription, for the resources you created in this book. This will delete all the artifacts created in Azure for this book.

Removing All Artifacts

When I was learning Azure, I was not deleting resources, even though I was really done with them. I also am a pack rat. These are bad things. The good thing to do, after you have read this book, is to delete the resources you created, or you will be racking up unnecessary charges. Soon, your free credit and/or your monthly credit will be used up! Using resource groups, as we have done in this book, makes this task very easy and quick.

Time Estimate

   5 Minutes

     1. In the Azure Management portal, click Resource groups. See Figure 6-1.

© Russell Fustino 2018
R. Fustino, *Azure and Xamarin Forms*, https://doi.org/10.1007/978-1-4842-3561-4_6

Figure 6-1. *Select Resource groups from your portal dashboard*

2. Click the resource group created in Chapter 4. It should be similar to BookPollAppRG resource group. Then select the Delete resource group action. See Figure 6-2.

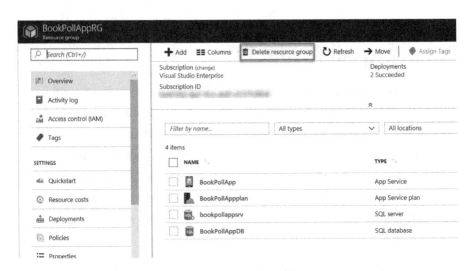

Figure 6-2. *Click Delete resource group*

3. If you have not already deleted the resources from Chapter 3, do so now as well. Delete the resources created in Chapter 3 by clicking on Resource groups and then pressing the Delete button for each of them. They should be called something similar to demorg, MYWebsiteRG, rgfromps, and SQL2018RG.

4. Click the Delete resource group button to delete the resource group. When prompted, type in the name of the resource group, to confirm. See Figure 6-3.

Figure 6-3. *Click Delete resource group for each resource group created in this book*

Summary

In this chapter, you have removed the related resources that were created in previous chapters.

Book Summary

In this book, you learned several important applications and concepts with which to create a working Xamarin Forms app and use Azure, including the following:

Xamarin Forms:

- Navigation

- Layout controls, such as StackLayout and GridLayout

- Device-dependent logic to adapt to phones and tablets

- File input and output

- Embedded resources by using images

- ListView template page and template customization

- A working Xamarin Forms app and an understanding of the solution structure

Azure:

- Azure portal, resource usage, and billing data

- High-level architecture from end to end, by creating a Virtual Machine, SQL database, ASP.NET web site, and a mobile app

- Deployment from GitHub

Azure and Xamarin Forms:

- Using the Azure Mobile Apps Quickstart template to create a database and create a service app with a Table API and a new sample Xamarin Forms app

- Consuming that service in the client application, by taking an existing app and modifying it to use Azure client services

- Creating offline storage with SQLite and synchronization with an online SQL database

- Using tools to verify database table data.

Note   The source code and assets for this book can be downloaded from `https://github.com/Apress/azure-and-xamarin-forms`

Index

Printed in the United States
By Bookmasters